Mother

The Pinnacle of Beauty

PEESAPATI CHANDRA SEKHAR

INDIA · SINGAPORE · MALAYSIA

Index

A Letter of Appreciation

Peesapati Chandra Sekhar is a successful short story writer and my childhood friend. In this novel he presented the concept of motherhood in a lucid expressive style.

Mother is our first teacher. She lives for the well-being of her children till her last breath. Her every movement, thoughts and deeds are targetted at the happiness of her children. She's the greatest lover, the highest sacrificer, the best guide and friend. Above all she is a wonderful psychologist. Motherhood is universal. Every creature comes out into this world through mother's womb. Mother is the only person on the earth with no enemies. She is the incarnation of God on the earth.

This book contains hundred chapters and each chapter depicts mother's sacred love towards all. She is an excellent lover of her husband. A true friend. A selfless servant. A wonderful companion. A sincere adviser. I wish every mother and every child should read this novel and remember his life's journey with his mother.

My heartfelt appreciations to Peesapati Chandra Sekhar for his wonderful presentation. I wish him many more applauses from all over the world for this beautiful work.

Dr. Nallamilli Sesha Reddy
Chancellor
Aditya University

The First Light

Salutations to the mother who gave me birth. This life is the result of her unparalleled sacrifice, standing at the brink of mortality to bring me into existence.

To my father, my guiding force and the divine seed of my birth, I offer my heartfelt gratitude. You both are embodiments of love, dwelling eternally in realms of joy and peace.

My existence is the fruit of your union, the outcome of your love and oneness. Forgetting the external world, you envisioned a new one, and I am the sacred result of that divine endeavor. One of you became the epitome of sacrifice, the other a fountain of compassion. From the moment I first touched this earth, you cradled me in your arms and nurtured me like a delicate flower, filling me with sweetness and grace. For this, I am eternally indebted to you both, unable to repay you in any way.

One of you became my eyes, the other my vision. One became the rhythm of my heart, the other my breath. One served me selflessly, the other protected me tirelessly. One laid the path before me, the other held my hand and guided me forward. Your care and guidance were like the sun and moon, illuminating my life and filling it with light.

My father, who stood as my protector and guide, has now journeyed to the divine realms. Like a star in the heavens, he continues to guide me, showering me with moonlit smiles from above. He filled my mother with his light before ascending, and now he blesses me with eternal smiles and grace.

The greatest treasure that God gave me is my mother, who continues to shower me with her boundless compassion. Like a magnificent cloud, she rains love and kindness upon me. Today, as she celebrates her 100th birthday, I find myself reflecting on how rare and divine a blessing it is to have such a mother—a gift that not every child is fortunate to receive.

I wish to give my mother a beautiful gift today. Till now, she has not expected anything from me. A woman who abandoned all material desires and wore happiness as her sole ornament—what could possibly suffice as a gift for her?

I want her to feel boundless joy when she sees my offering. I want to be uplifted with divine bliss upon witnessing her happiness. The gift I present must be unparalleled in the world. It must be something that neither wealth nor strength can acquire, something unique that no one has ever created—a creation as sacred as a devotee's dance of devotion to God. But how?

I pondered deeply for days, and my heart brimmed with love. It churned like a vast ocean, and the nectar of your love for me revealed the answer. By your grace, I have completed eighty springs of life. Along this journey, I have gathered the sweetest memories of our bond, like flowers strung into a garland, and given them the form of words.

I have crafted this humble collection of letters as an offering to place at your feet. With this, I wish to bow my head at your lotus feet and express my gratitude. Please accept this with grace, dear mother, and shower me with your blessings.

Supreme Beauty

That was a full Moon day. I was wandering in the wide greenish fields. A lovely and wonderful night it was. The bright Moon light was reflecting on the lands, making everything clearly visible.

I looked up at the silver Moon. It seemed that the Moon was very happily sprinkling her cool and lovely rays on the Earth. On one side a large group of poets gathered and were ready to write beautiful poems. They were all well prepared with pens and papers of multiple colors. They were continually moving their heads up and down, fully immersed in giving vent to their creativity.

Singers, both male and female were sitting in a row and started singing songs of love and romance at different scales. Young lovers were moving in the fields, hand in hand. Their feet were touching the ground, but their souls were dancing above the skies. They were looking almost like the birds of love flying with joy. Pretty and alluring creepers on the ground were looking like a living beauty with fully covered lovely flowers.

Very venomous cobras shining brightly in the Moonlight were entwining themselves into pairs, dancing and mating with deep emotions.

I wondered looking at those beauties around; understood that all that was because of one single heavenly object called the Moon. What a wonderful picture it was to watch! What an aesthetic feast to the eyes! Immediately I concluded and resolved 'There is no other creation in the universe than the Moon that can gift both beauty and happiness in a single pack to the human world.'

I wanted to tell my Mother describing the supreme and mesmerizing beauty of the Moon and Moon light. I wanted my

Mother to come to that spot and watch the beauties directly. I was sure that my Mother will definitely be thrilled and will dance heartily in ultimate joy.

I ran quickly towards my house to invite my Mother. My Mother was standing at the door awaiting me. Her lips were silent. But her eyes questioned me – 'Where are you from and why are you so hurried'?

I watched her dazzling face. Stood still, like a statue, without words. 'Oh my God!' my Mother's face was a thousand times more radiant than that of the Moon. Her smile was much more captivating than the Moon light. 'If the Moon is able to see, she will feel defeated and bend her face in shame.' I thought.

I wanted to run back to the fields and bring all the poets to my house. I was sure that they would throw away all their poems on the Moon and would write wonderful verses on my Mother. All the singers would run towards my Mother and sing new songs praising her charming and ineffable divine beauty and grace. The lovers would dance with undreamt of delight. The children would circle around my Mother and frolic in overwhelming bliss and joy. All the beauties in the fields would personify themselves as divine Goddesses and worship my Mother with utmost devotion. They would pray to my Mother to grant at least some of her magical charms as permanent gifts to them.

'My Mother's face is brighter than the Moon. She is beyond comparison to anyone and anything else on the Earth. Unlike the Moon, she is a spotless beauty. She is a Moon moving in and around the Earth.

The Moon in the sky shines very brightly, but only once in a month. My Mother is majestically divine and radiant at every moment. The Moon is a lifeless material object. My Mother is the omnipresent and omniscient divine force. She loves and is loved by all. The Moon reflects the radiance of the Sun. My Mother is self effulgent person on the Earth.

So far, I thought that the Moon was the Supreme beauty. But after keenly and attentively observing, realization downed on me that the real and the most supreme beauty is my Mother'.

I ran back in a kind of trance to the fields to bring all of them and present them before my Mother.

Everyone there turned towards me in surprise. They lifted their eyebrows questioning me about the new radiance in me. I stood thrilled and was incapable of understanding what I was going through. I was totally embarrassed at their unexpected reactions. I went there with a lot to speak, but I was speechless. Instead, they started questioning me all about the sudden revelations they were witnessing and experiencing. I was totally confused out of blue. It was a sudden spiritual experience hitherto unknown to me.

'What are these new scintillations on your face? Where from they emerged suddenly'?

'Who has granted these ineffable and sweet smiles to you'?

'How is it possible that you are looking more charming than you were a few minutes before'?

'So far we have run after the Moon and written wonderful poems. Now you are more graceful and gorgeous than the Moon. What shall we do now'?

There were many more questions from each and every corner of the fields. I was baffled for a while. Slowly, I realized the reasons for my transformation. The answer to all those questions flashed in my mind. A single word echoed amusingly - 'Mother'. Yes. My mother was the reason. The grace, love, charm and radiance from my Mother made me a totally new charming being.

What a wonderful gift is 'Mother'! Every moment spent in her presence brightens the souls of the children. A moving God on the Earth she is. 'O Dear Mother! How can I show my gratitude for the eternally lasting great virtues you bestowed upon me- except by bowing myself before and resting my head in your lap and prostrating to your Lotus feet'

The Master Sculptor Who Carved Me

I woke up early in the morning. After drinking a big glass of warm, delicious milk my mother gave me, I stepped outside. The orange-hued sun greeted me with a warm smile from the sky.

Walking leisurely, I reached the edge of a pond. The neem tree nearby, its lush branches swaying in the cool breeze, seemed to welcome me. I sat beneath its shade, inhaling the pure air deeply and feeling immense joy.

From a nearby temple, the resonant chimes of bells echoed, lasting for about a minute. The sound felt as if celestial beings descended to Earth to recite sacred hymns in the presence of the Divine. Drawn by the sound, I walked toward the temple and stepped inside. A beautiful, divine idol came into view, leaving me entranced for several moments. Such a glorious figure! I thought, "What a remarkable sculptor must have created this masterpiece!"

Continuing my walk, I reached a vast open area. From within, I heard the harmonious chants of prayers. Entering the hall, I found myself in a temple bathed in divine light. A large cross stood prominently, inviting everyone to gather. Nearby, an exquisite sculpture of Christ, radiating compassion and grace, caught my eye. With devotion, I closed my eyes for a moment. When I opened them, I gazed at the figure in awe and thought, "Ah! The sculptor who created this form of divine mercy must truly be blessed!"

My steps carried me further, eventually pausing at another spot. I heard the heartfelt cries of "Allah! Allah!" Entering inside, I saw hundreds of worshippers bowing reverently. Observing the beautiful architecture, I felt awe and wondered, "Who could be the brilliant craftsman behind this magnificent creation?"

With these thoughts swirling in my mind, I came across a sage meditating peacefully under a tree. Bowing at his feet, I asked, "Swami, is the sculpture greater, or the sculptor?"

"The sculptor is greater than the sculpture," he replied. "Greater still is the supreme sculptor who created us and this entire universe. All the divine places you've visited are meant to direct your gaze toward that ultimate sculptor."

"Who is this master sculptor? Where can I find him? I wish to see him," I said earnestly.

"No one has ever seen him directly, my child," the sage replied. "But he watches over us and protects us. By day, he appears as the sun, and by night, as the moon."

I left the sage and headed home. Along the way, I glanced at the sky repeatedly. The radiant sun seemed to be following me, and I wondered, "Could this be the master sculptor?" I spent the day pondering this question, watching as the sun gradually set.

At night, lying on a cot in the courtyard, I gazed at the sky. The full moon, like a blossoming jasmine flower, smiled down at me, its cool light descending gently as though it had come just for me. "Could this be the master sculptor watching over me?" I wondered.

No matter how much I thought, neither the sun nor the moon could evoke a profound emotion in my heart. I returned to the sage and poured out my confusion.

The sage took my hand and led me somewhere. Like a calf following its mother, I obediently accompanied him. Surprisingly, he brought me back home and locked me inside, saying, "Stay here. Do not leave. You will find him here." With that, he departed.

At first, I resisted, thinking, "How will I see the sun and the moon if I remain indoors?" Yet, trusting his wisdom, I decided to follow his instructions.

I spent the entire day with my mother. Every time she approached me, I felt a divine energy radiating from her. Her warmth, gentle gaze, and nurturing presence stirred my heart deeply. It felt as though I were floating in the cool glow of moonlight while dancing amidst a radiant light. It was like beholding both the sun and the moon together in the sky.

My mother stood before me, her right eye shining like a thousand suns, and left eye exuding the soothing calm of moonlight. She gazed at me with such tenderness that it moved me to tears.

"Are you the master sculptor who created, nurtured, and shaped me, Mother?" I thought. "How blind I have been all these years, wandering through hills and valleys in search of a divine presence, while ignoring the divinity before me."

Filled with gratitude, I silently thanked the sage for revealing this eternal truth. Bowing my head at my mother's feet, I offered my reverence and felt truly blessed.

———•———

The Light That Glimmered at the Edge of Darkness

Steps were falling—step after uncertain step. Along unseen paths, through a maze of disordered trails, my feet moved tirelessly. I walked on and on, ceaselessly, without knowing where I was headed. What began in a faint glow soon merged into dense, impenetrable darkness. Everything vanished from sight. Stretching my arms into the void, fumbling through the blackness, I continued forward.

This was a journey chosen by none but myself—toward an unknown destination, along an uncharted path. I wandered invisibly on a trail where the sun did not rise. Hoping for a sign, I raised my gaze, but the stars offered no guidance. There was no moonlight to brighten my hopes. Slowly, fear crept in. My body, though unseen, was drenched in sweat.

Who pushed me into this abyss? Was it my arrogance? My ignorance? In the suffocating darkness, I cried out, "Is anyone there?" But my voice echoed unanswered as I wandered aimlessly.

Exhaustion overtook me. My steps, though heavy, dragged me forward. How long had I been walking? Moments? Hours? Days? I had no sense of time. My cheeks burned as something slid past them. Tears—they flowed unchecked, drowning me like an endless river. I felt weightless, adrift like a withered leaf in a storm. My voice faltered, my cries incoherent. Lost in despair, I floated aimlessly.

Far in the distance, a small glimmer of light appeared. What was it? Hope? Slowly, the suffocating darkness began to loosen its grip. Drawn to the tiny speck, I moved toward it. The light, once faint, grew brighter. To my astonishment, it expanded, transforming into a radiant moon. Spreading its silver beams, it seemed to invite me lovingly, saying, "Come closer." Afraid it might vanish if I blinked, I ran with all my might. Delaying even a moment felt like an eternity wasted.

And then, the revelation struck. What I had seen was not a star, not the moon. It was my mother. Those weren't beams of moonlight—they were the radiant smiles of my mother. The hope I had discovered, the light that guided me, was my mother. My journey's end was my mother. Completely drained, I rushed to her and collapsed at her feet.

She touched my shoulder, lifted me up, wiped my tear-streaked cheeks, and stroked my head lovingly. Pulling me close, she held me in a perfect embrace, her warmth filling me with new strength. As she spoke to me with infinite love, she guided me forward—to a new world, resplendent with the brilliance of a thousand suns.

Our conversation went like this:

"Mother, darkness is so terrifying."

"Darkness is also very good, my child."

"But darkness is frightening, Mother."

"Only through fear will you search for courage."

"Darkness is ignorance, isn't it, Mother?"

"It is the foundation of knowledge, my child."

"Why did you appear at the end, Mother? Why didn't you warn me about the darkness earlier?"

"That path was your choice, my dear. Understanding the truths and falsehoods along it was your journey to make. That is a great fortune in itself. You didn't get lost in the darkness—you kept walking. You are my very breath; how could I ever leave you? I was waiting for you, always."

From that moment on, I never left my mother's side, and she never let go of my hand. Through every dark forest I encountered, she scattered flowers on my path. In the vast ocean where no shore was in sight, she became my guiding star, showing me the way.

A mother is an immeasurable blessing to human life. The absence of a mother is an unbearable curs

The Rare Wishing Tree

Mother, my life has been a treasure trove of blessings. The rare and divine force that laid bundles of fortune at my feet and guided me through every step of life is you. In moments of solitude, I often flip through the pages of my life's book, reading and reminiscing. You've been my guiding star, standing by me like my shadow, reading my mind even before I could, and shielding me from worries. You are my priceless Chintamani (the wish-fulfilling gem).

Many friends have often shared their grievances with me, saying, "Our lives are filled with hardships." When I asked them what hardships were, they would laugh at me, envying the cheerful glow on my face. One day, I asked you, "Mother, what is hardship?" Even today, your words echo sweetly in my ears like the strings of a veena:

"Hardship is a wicked force that burdens our lives and minds. But it will never reach you. It has not touched you, and it never will as long as I am here."

Now, I realize that you are the embodiment of love who shielded me from every hardship. You ensured my eyes shed tears only out of joy, never sorrow. You shaped me into a brave traveler who walks through life fearlessly, never bowing to any circumstance. You are my divine sculptor. Truly, you are the Chintamani, filling my life with boundless light and love.

I wandered through beautiful forests, admiring their splendor. I felt the sweetness of your breath in the cool breeze. The flowers, like your radiant smile, greeted and thrilled me. The tender branches, swaying gently, caressed my cheeks like your soft, loving hands, urging me forward. The rustling of leaves in the wind felt like the lullabies you sang, delighting my ears and heart.

For a moment, I was transported back to childhood, to those sweet moments spent in your lap, playing with you, sharing laughter. But then, my thoughts stopped abruptly, and I realized the forest could never truly compare to you. The beauty of these woods lasts only in spring, but you are eternal, my Kalpataru (the wishing tree). You are not just a tree that bears fruit; you are the divine tree that bears fruit in all seasons, spreading joy and fulfillment. The joy I felt in the forest was fleeting, but the eternal bliss I experience with you is unmatched.

Running back, I rested at your feet. Immersed in your eternal love, I found solace and realized a truth:

"Why do you shine so brightly within me, Mother?"

"You are my wishing tree, Mother. You are my true sanctuary."

You smiled softly, held my hand, and lifted me up. Leading me along, you pointed to a corner where my father, serene and tireless, was laboring like a devoted farmer.

"If I am a wishing tree," you said, "it is because of him. He nurtured and raised me with care, so I could provide you with shade and fruit. He is the embodiment of love, the foundation of my life. For my sake, he pours out his sweat and transforms it into comfort for us. He is the divine being who spins a protective web of love around us. Both of you, my child, are the heartbeat of my life. You both are my very breath."

My eyes filled with tears, and my vision blurred. "Children blessed with parents like you are truly the rarest of all treasures!"

The Unread Reader

One day, upon a friend's invitation, I went to attend a celebration at his home. He welcomed me with great joy, embraced me warmly, and led me inside. Introducing me to everyone as his dearest friend, he made me feel like one of their own. The joy I felt was indescribable.

After the festivities, a grand feast was arranged. My friend sat beside me, eagerly encouraging me to try various dishes. Everything was new and different, unlike the familiar taste of my mother's cooking. I found the flavors unusual and asked him what they were. As he explained each dish, I felt my throat tighten. A strange unease swept over me. No amount of water could quench the burning in my mind.

I excused myself to wash my hands and stepped away. My thoughts spiraled:

"Must so many animals lose their lives just to satisfy a person's hunger? Should rivers of blood flow for the pleasure of taste? Should one creature's joy come at the cost of another's life?"

Why am I thinking this way? Others seemed to be enjoying the feast without a second thought. My friend called out to me, but my steps led me back home.

Seeing the distress on my face, my mother asked what had happened. I explained everything and asked her, "Why, Mother? Why do people find joy in this?"

Mother responded with a gentle smile:

"Fish live in water, birds in the air, animals in the forest, and humans in societies. Each being has its own food and its own joy."

"If this is their joy, why didn't you ever offer it to me from my childhood?" I asked.

"Your tongue may crave taste, but your body needs health. To me, your well-being matters the most. That's why I could never offer you that kind of joy. Your mind is unsettled now. There's a pond near the prayer hall on the edge of the village. Drink water from it—it will calm your mind. While returning, take the royal road and observe carefully."

I did as she advised. When I returned, I asked her for an explanation. She smiled and said, "Tell me, child, who and what did you see along your path?"

"Mother," I began, "I saw strange sights. People shouting and insulting each other, some even fighting. I saw aimless wanderers with lost minds, faces devoid of happiness, burdened by worry. There were thieves and robbers. There were doctors with outstretched hands, calling people for treatment. But in one corner, I saw some animals peacefully resting after their meal, enjoying their time. These sights have left an impression on my mind, but I don't know how to make sense of them. That's why I've come to you for answers."

Mother placed a comforting hand on my shoulder and said,

"My dear child, I raised you in a way that protected you from worry, hatred, conflicts, greed, and even small ailments requiring a doctor. The path you walked today is new, the life you've led so far is unique. Your journey has been one of purity."

"Why, Mother? Why did you raise me this way?"

"Every human body has six vital energy centers that tirelessly work for us. These are called 'chakras' by our elders because they constantly spin with activity. Your digestion must work well. Your excretory system must function properly. Your breathing must be steady. Your speech must be clear. Your thoughts must be balanced. As long as these six centers operate harmoniously, your mind will dance in joy. Such a person doesn't just live as a human but thrives as a 'Maneeshi' (a wise soul). My wish was to raise you into such a person. You've fulfilled my wish."

"What about the others, Mother?" I asked.

"Each person's dietary habits and lifestyle are their own, my child. Whether you live in serene bliss with purity, burn with restless ambition, or sink into ignorance is entirely your choice. These three—Sattva, Rajas, and Tamas—intertwine, and no one is free from their influence. We cannot judge others, my dear."

"Mother," I said hesitantly, "I've never asked you this before, but I feel like asking now. What did you study? Which school did you go to?"

"I never studied, my child. My mother's lap was my school. I walked the path she showed me, and I guided you on that very path."

"What a beautiful legacy, Mother! Every child has a responsibility to preserve such a treasure. As your son, I feel deeply blessed to have you as my mother."

—·—·—●—·—·—·—

The Bundle of Riches

A marvelous dance was in progress. A gathering of exquisite beauties swayed and sang in ecstasy, their presence rivaling the radiance of celestial beings. Decked in golden ornaments adorned with dazzling diamonds, they sparkled like stars, basking in their own brilliance.

Amidst their mesmerizing performance, you appeared, mother. Instantly, the rhythm stopped. All eyes turned toward you, their gazes questioning, their movements frozen. A voice emerged from the group, "Why have you come among us? Do you think you match us? Do you possess the riches to stand equal to us? You are a simple woman with no adornments. You don't belong here. Leave!"

They humiliated you, Mother. I felt small, unsure of what to say or do. I glanced at you with apprehension, only to find a serene calmness on your face, glowing like the soft light of a Sharad Purnima moon (full moon in autumn).

With a steady voice, you declared, "I have brought my bundle of riches with me."

Their brows furrowed in confusion. "Show us your riches!" they demanded. You pointed to me and said, "This is my bundle of riches."

A wave of mockery swept through the group. Their whispers grew louder, their laughter scornful. They wanted to insult you, diminish you. But your unshaken smile only deepened their envy.

Drawing me close, you rested my face against yours. In that instant, a brilliant light radiated from our eyes, as if diamonds had begun to sparkle. "See the brilliance of my diamonds," you said. Then, gently stroking my cheeks with love, you added, "These are my precious gems." You wrapped my arms around your neck. "This is the golden garland adorning me," you said with pride.

Overcome with love for you, I placed my arms around your waist. "Look at the rubies that embellish my girdle," you continued.

"These are no ordinary riches," you said, your voice steady and triumphant. "Your riches lack life. They sparkle only when light falls upon them. My riches are alive. They shine eternally, filling my life with joy. Bind your lifeless riches into bundles and cast them into the river," you concluded with a laugh, your radiant smile glimmering like a string of pearls.

Taking your hand, I turned with you. "Pearls are falling from my mother's lips," I called to the others. "Gather them if you wish."

I knew, Mother. Behind us, their faces would have twisted with anger, their spirits crumbled under the weight of humiliation. But you stood tall, majestic like a queen, basking in the joy of victory.

"Arrogant woman!" a loud voice bellowed from the group.

The crowd retreated, their steps hurried like the thundering wheels of a racing train. We walked forward, our steps light, like a vibrant boat drifting joyfully across a sea of happiness.

"Mother, are you arrogant?" I asked.

"Any mother who holds a bundle of riches like you, my child, has every right to be proud!"

My fingers tightened around your hand in a loving grip. You walked with a purpose, and I followed, walking by your side... and I continue to walk, always by your side.

—·—·—●—·—·—

The Divine Within the Heart

A beautiful path stretched before me, lined with blooming trees whose fragrance filled the air, welcoming me with a gentle embrace. Petals fell in abundance, spreading a soft carpet, as if urging me forward. I set off on this seemingly endless floral path. Beginning my journey at twilight, I was enraptured by the splendor of the world around me. Birds soared and played in unison, their joy mirroring the beauty of the scene. It felt as though all of nature was walking alongside me, following me with affection.

Turning back, I noticed the path behind me disappearing. Looking ahead, the destination was shrouded in mystery. Amid this wonder, the Sun emerged from between the trees, casting his golden light as if in friendly competition with me. I walked all day until he bid farewell, sinking into the western horizon. From the eastern hills, the full moon rose, its glow encouraging me to continue. I pressed on, conversing with nature's beauty along the way.

Who is the magnificent creator who conjured such an awe-inspiring world? What does he look like? Can I ever see him? Speak with him? Express my gratitude?

Days under the warm sunlight and nights beneath the cool moonlight passed as I walked. How long will this journey last? Where is it taking me? Will my questions ever find answers? Is there someone who can fulfill my longing?

I stopped before a place of prayer and asked, "Who is the creator of this universe?" The reply came, "He is the Supreme Being, the origin, the protector, and the ultimate destroyer."

"Have you seen him? Touched him? Spoken to him?" I asked. Silence followed. Disheartened, I moved on.

At another sacred place, I asked the same question. "He is the guardian of all beings. He guides you and protects you. He is compassion incarnate," came the answer.

"Have you seen him? Touched him? Spoken to him?" Silence again. With growing despair, I continued my search.

At a serene temple, I knelt and repeated my questions. "He is the divine energy sustaining you, a loving force nurturing and protecting you," they said. Once again, silence was the response to my follow-up questions. Once again, disappointment pushed me onward.

I looked up at the sky, dotted with stars. I realized I was engulfed in darkness, with no end in sight. With unanswered questions weighing on my soul, I raced forward like a tireless seeker.

Suddenly, a new light dawned. In the distance, a glorious golden mountain glimmered, inviting me like a throne of a celestial emperor. Running toward it, I climbed to the summit, my body tingling with an unfamiliar sensation.

"I have seen God. I have touched God. I have spoken to God!" I proclaimed loudly, my voice echoing across the hills.

Thousands of devotees surrounded the mountain, gazing at me with astonishment. The elders I had met earlier approached, their faces alight with curiosity.

"How did you see the God we could not? What does he look like? How did he touch you and fill you with such bliss? Tell us, please!" they urged.

I spoke with conviction: "The God who breathed life into the tiniest cell is the same God who gave me form. For nine months, He nurtured me in a sacred space, protecting me as if I were the pupil of

His eye. He endured indescribable pain to bring me into this world. He gave me breath, made me human, and walked with me every step of the way. That God is none other than my mother. She is my true God.

Friends, the Creator of the universe is an invisible force, a formless entity. He cannot be confined to a physical form or gender. He exists as the essence of life in every being—in creatures, plants, and animals. To make Himself accessible to us ordinary mortals, He manifests as mother. Without her, there is no birth, no life, no existence.

Look no further than your own mother to see God. Touch her feet with love and speak to her with affection. She watches over you tirelessly, waiting for you. Go home, seek your mothers, and worship the divine in her."

The crowd dispersed, running to their homes. The three elders exchanged glances, smiled knowingly, nodded in agreement, and disappeared into thin air.

A soft whisper resonated in my heart—it was the sound of your gentle laughter, Mother. It was the sacred blessing of your divine presence flowing like a holy river through me.

A Living Portrait

"Mother, you are alone. Age is catching up with you. As time passes, you may reach a point where you need help. The time has come for me to care for you, just as you have cared for me since my first breath. Come with me, Mother. Stay with me. From now on, every moment of my life will be dedicated to your happiness. Being with you will fill my days with joy. Come, leave this small cottage and this village behind, and be with me."

You listened patiently to my heartfelt plea. Smiling like a blossoming flower, you shook your head—not vertically as you always did to grant my wishes, but horizontally in quiet refusal. Taking my hand, you led me through your little cottage, showing me its surroundings with delight.

"This is the hut your father built," you said. "Every corner of it is infused with his sweat and love. It is the temple he created for me. I cannot leave this sacred place. This cottage is my breath. Without it, I cannot live. Here, his presence surrounds me, whispering to me, guiding me.

It is true, leaving you would be hard, but leaving this house of love would be impossible. You think I am alone, but I am not. Though he is no longer here physically, his spirit fills me with strength. His memories are my breath. Here, we continue to speak and walk together, enjoying the breeze by the pond, swinging on the tree branches, and playing with the animals. How can I leave all this? If I leave, that is when I will truly become alone."

Without words, I bowed my head and decided to honor your wish.

I invited a great artist from the city to paint your portrait. He was renowned for bringing life to his work, praised as a modern-day Ravi Varma. When I told you my plan, your eyes questioned me, asking, "Why?"

"I want your portrait, Mother," I explained. "I will keep it with me and worship you as my God."

"My portrait?" you asked, smiling. "It would only reflect my body. Can it capture the depths of my soul? Can it depict the love I feel for you? The words I long to share with you? The joy my heart feels whenever I think of you? No painting can convey that. If you need such a picture, create it yourself."

I was speechless, humbled by your words. How foolish I was to think of confining the goddess within you to a lifeless painting! You, who live in my breath, who fill my life with love and light—how could I think of reducing you to a mere image?

"True bonds are not tied by physical form," you said. "They are woven by the connection of hearts. Such a bond is real, eternal, and divine."

Your words remain etched in my soul. Whether my eyes are open or closed, your sacred form dances before me. Even when we are apart, I can feel your presence, your love, and your guidance. You are my Sun, my eternal light. My respectful salutations to you, my mother.

The Joy of Defeat

I returned home, elated, clutching a prestigious award I had just won. Brimming with excitement, I wanted to share my joy with you. I placed the trophy at your feet and recounted my triumph in vivid detail, overwhelmed by my own achievement.

You looked at me with a gentle smile, your expression calm and unchanged. Without a word about my victory, you brought me a warm glass of milk. "You must be tired. Drink this and sit down to rest," you said softly.

"Mother! Doesn't my success mean anything to you? Does this award not make you happy? It's a rare achievement, earned by defeating many others. Why doesn't it bring you joy?" I exclaimed, bewildered.

Once again, you smiled serenely.

"Winning by defeating others brings success, my child, but not true joy. Try lifting others who are struggling. Help those in pain, comfort those in sorrow, and support those who are lost. That is where real happiness lies. Once you taste that happiness, you will yearn to live it every day. You will find yourself addicted to the joy of helping others win. It will fill you with treasures far greater than any award. The light of that joy will shine in your heart, and I will see its radiance in you. Share your love, my child, and it will spread across the world."

Her words pierced my heart. My vision blurred as tears welled up in my eyes. For a moment, everything went dark. Slowly, the fog lifted, and I saw the truth with newfound clarity. Could there really be greater joy in helping others succeed? Is the happiness of others the source of our own true happiness? What a profound truth! Was this the essence of motherhood?

I looked for you, but you weren't there. Searching, I found you by a pond at the edge of the village, sitting peacefully. Your face radiated waves of contentment. Silently, I knelt beside you, watching.

You held a small bowl of food, feeding it bit by bit to the fish in the pond. They gathered eagerly, their tails swaying with joy as they devoured the meal. "Did you notice their happiness?" you asked me. "Did you see their gratitude, their love as they wagged their tails and looked at us with moist eyes?"

For the first time, I glimpsed a beautiful new world. The tender emotion in the eyes of those simple creatures moved me deeply. How could such a poetic moment escape notice? Even the greatest poets would bow before the profound compassion of a mother.

From there, you disappeared. Searching again, I found you near a rocky slope. Running toward you, I asked, "Mother! The sun is scorching. What are you doing here?"

You gestured for me to sit beside you. A short distance away, a woman was breaking stones under the blazing sun, her body drenched in sweat. Yet, when her baby cried from hunger, she immediately stopped her work. Running to the tree where a cradle hung, she picked up her child, cradling it to her chest. Feeding the baby, her exhaustion faded, replaced by a serene joy as she smiled lovingly at her child.

I turned to you for answers, but you were gone. Only your voice remained: "Keep walking, child, and return home when you are ready."

I followed your words as my guide. I continue to walk, Mother, carrying your lessons in my heart.

Through my journey, I've learned countless truths, always remembering you. You taught me the greatness of giving over receiving, the fulfillment of sharing over accumulating. To my first teacher, who illuminated my life with these eternal lessons, I offer my deepest respects as I continue reading the pages of life's endless book.

1 + 1 = 1

"Mother, what does Father do?" I once asked you.

"He does many things," you replied.

But I didn't understand. So, driven by curiosity, I decided to find out for myself. I insisted on accompanying him, despite his reluctance. Finally, holding my hand, he took me along.

As we walked, people gathered to meet him. With reverence, they made way for him, bowing and greeting him with respect. "You are our protector," they said. "We thrive under your care." Why did everyone regard him so highly? Was he a king?

He ascended a high seat, listening to petitions, resolving disputes, issuing warnings, and giving commands. "This is justice; respect it," he said. Was he a judge?

Later, he entered a garden. He dug the soil, watered the plants, pruned the leaves, admired the blooming flowers, and shared the harvested fruits with joy. Was he a gardener?

Sweat trickled down his face as he toiled tirelessly. Was he a laborer?

Standing amidst a vast crowd, he shone like a beacon of hope. He comforted the distressed, visited the sick, clothed the destitute, encouraged the timid, and honored the brave. Was he a savior?

To the lustful, he preached restraint. To the angry, he offered calmness. To the greedy, he taught generosity. To the proud, he showed humility. His wisdom cleansed deluded minds, and his compassion healed jealous hearts.

I was amazed by his multifaceted personality. Immersed in his duties, he shone brightly, like the sun radiating light. As a leader, protector, teacher, and friend, he was an inspiration.

I resolved never to let go of his hand. As evening fell, we returned home together.

But to my astonishment, the father who had shone like the sun outside transformed into the moon at home. He became gentle, loving, and calm—a friend, a servant, and a comforting presence who filled the house with serenity. How could one person change so effortlessly?

"Father, why this transformation?" I asked.

"This is not my domain, my son. This is your mother's kingdom. It deserves our respect," he replied.

What a profound truth! How many conflicts and misunderstandings could be avoided if this were universally understood!

Though the three of us lived under one roof, my thoughts made me feel alone. A question stirred within me, keeping me awake that night:

"Who is greater—Father or Mother? Who wins this game of love?"

No matter how much I analyzed, they complemented each other perfectly. They were not opponents but halves of the same whole.

Late at night, my gaze fell on their sleeping forms. Mother rested her head on Father's shoulder, while Father lay motionless to avoid disturbing her. What a beautiful sight! Two souls, inseparable in their unity.

Exhausted by my deliberation, I finally drifted into sleep. In my dreams, Mother appeared. Beside her stood Father. Then Father appeared, with Mother by his side. The answer became clear: they complete each other.

1 + 1 = 1.

Content and at peace, I fell into a deep, fulfilling sleep.

Infinite Love

In a serene garden blooming with vibrant flowers, my father sat on a high pedestal, playing the flute. The melody was so mesmerizing that nature itself seemed to pause and listen. Birds stopped fluttering their wings, flowers and leaves swayed gently, and even grazing cattle ceased their chewing, turning their heads to the divine music. Venomous serpents emerged from their burrows, spreading their hoods, swaying rhythmically as if in a trance. I stood there, entranced by this extraordinary sight.

The waves of music filled the air, caressing my ears with their divine beauty. Suddenly, I heard the tinkling sound of anklets approaching. A group of celestial beauties, radiant like apsaras, gathered to listen to my father's music. Their exquisite beauty lit up the surroundings as they sat silently, enthralled by the ethereal notes.

The silence deepened, and the enchanting music wove its magic, blending seamlessly with the stillness. My father, immersed in his melody, slowly opened his eyes. The celestial women, who had been gazing at him with unblinking eyes, shyly lowered their gazes. Some approached him and sat at his feet, others leaned on his lap with reverence, and a few touched him with adoration, lost in devotion. My father, calm and radiant, acknowledged them all with a gentle smile. He looked like a divine being among his admirers.

The scene was captivating, yet an unease began to stir within me. How could my father, with so many women around him, act like this when Mother was at home? It felt wrong. Without hesitation, I ran home and grabbed my mother's hand, pulling her toward the garden. I was ready to expose my father.

Father looked at Mother, stretched out his hand to welcome her, and explained, "These women have come here for me. They admire me, they revere me, and they return here every day." His words shocked me. How could he speak so boldly? I grew angry. Surely Mother would feel the same!

But to my surprise, she didn't. Instead of anger, she responded with a serene smile. Showering even more affection than Father, she warmly greeted the women. Walking among them, she addressed each by name, praised their talents, and conversed with genuine interest.

The celestial women, who had been glowing with pride moments before, now looked pale and subdued. Quietly, they retreated the way they had come, leaving me utterly bewildered. How could Mother remain so composed? How could she accept this? Did she forgive him so easily? Was she truly this good-hearted?

On the way back home, my mind raced with questions.

"Mother, didn't you feel angry? Didn't you want to confront those women for their audacity? Weren't you afraid Father might drift away from you? Didn't you feel even a trace of jealousy seeing him surrounded by so many beautiful women?"

Mother smiled, but her smile wasn't enough for me. I repeated my questions more insistently.

"Your father is a universal lover," she began. "His heart is vast enough to embrace everything around him. He loves not just those women but the entire creation. Did you not notice the trees, the animals, the birds, and even the serpents—how they were all enchanted by his music, pulsing with life and joy? Why weren't you angry at them?"

"Love isn't a tiny drop, my dear—it's an infinite ocean. You asked if I was afraid. Why should I be? Everyone may adore your father and he may love everyone, but he worships only me. His heart doesn't dwell with him—it resides in the temple within my chest. So tell me, why should either of us be afraid?"

At that moment, Mother seemed as vast as the sky itself, her boundless greatness leaving me awestruck. Overwhelmed with admiration, I followed her, step by step, trying to match her grace.

The True Source of Beauty

In a vast meadow, countless beautiful women gathered, their radiance akin to blooming flowers spreading sweet fragrances. Their golden hues sparkled like sunlight, their youthful elegance captivating the very essence of nature. Despite being together, each stood out with unique charm, their eyes filled with anticipation as they paced gracefully, waiting for someone.

Whom were they waiting for? Why were their gazes restless? It was clear—their beloveds were the focus of their longing. The language of their eyes spoke volumes, echoing their heartfelt yearning.

Their thoughts revolved around their lovers. "Come quickly," they seemed to plead silently. "Lay my heart's lotus upon the throne of your love. Hold me close, shelter me from these chilly winds. Cool my burning body with your gaze. Let your sweet words pour honey into my ears." Moving around the meadow, their every step and thought was consumed by their yearning.

Minutes turned to hours, but their beloveds did not appear. Others walked by—young men, but none seemed to notice these enchanting women. "We are here for you!" the women called out, but their cries went unheard.

The waiting stretched on endlessly. The pain of separation burned deeply. "Has our love been in vain? Have our hearts been wounded by fate? Is this reality or a terrible dream?" they wondered.

The sun, watching them with compassion, hid behind the clouds, yet their despair grew heavier. Their bodies began to wither under the weight of disappointment. Frustration turned to sorrow.

In their dismay, they tore off their jewelry and scattered their adornments on the ground.

"Our lovers don't care for us. They feel no love, no compassion for us. What's the use of waiting? Let us return home and drown in tears, mourning our unrequited love."

Suddenly, silence enveloped the meadow. A gentle breeze caressed their weary faces, and the faint sound of anklets reached their ears. Curious, they turned to look. Before them stood a woman—Mother.

Without a word, her eyes called out to them, her heart extended a warm invitation. "Who is she?" they asked each other, bewildered. "Our mother," one murmured. "No, she is ours," another protested. Drawn to her, they all rushed to her side.

"What happened?" she asked gently. Listening to their grievances, she wiped their tears, spoke words of comfort, and touched them with love. She breathed new hope into their weary hearts, instilled patience, and revived their dreams. Then, with a serene grace, she walked away, leaving them in awe.

A sudden commotion stirred behind them. They turned to see their beloveds approaching, their chests held high with pride.

"Beloved!" the women cried, rushing to their lovers' embrace. "How beautiful you are! How lucky I am!" their lovers exclaimed, holding them close.

The women, now radiant with joy, wondered aloud, "Why did our beauty, unnoticed before, suddenly captivate them? What miracle brought about this change? Who blessed us with this fortune?"

Realization dawned. "It was Mother's compassionate gaze that transformed us. Her words breathed new life into us, illuminating a beauty we had forgotten. Mother, we were so proud of our looks, so blinded by vanity that we lost sight of you, the very source of all we are. You, who gave us this beauty as a blessing, are our true miracle. We are blessed to have you."

With tears of gratitude, they rested in their lovers' embrace, cherishing the infinite beauty bestowed upon them by their Mother.

Fortune Vs Misfortune

"You gave me a form, brought me into existence, filled me with breath, and gifted me this vast, beautiful world. You stood by me, a shadow and shield, guarding me at every step. Did I ever ask for any of this, Mother? Were these not treasures you bestowed upon me, unasked, from the limitless depths of your love?" Who else on this earth, except a mother, gives everything without being asked?

You are the greatest reader of my heart, knowing its every word better than I do. Even in moments when I didn't know what I needed, your intuitive love filled the void and brought me comfort. The first drops of your milk sanctified me, nurturing not just my body but my soul. You soothed my hunger with your tender touch, taught me words sweeter than honey, and guided my faltering steps with your steady hand. Your eyes stayed open, watching over me until mine closed in sleep. When I awoke, you were always there, your face the first light my eyes met.

I cannot call this your strength, for strength often carries power and pride. What you have is something beyond—an endless cascade of love, pure and unselfish, flowing only for me.

From the moment I became aware, peace has been my constant companion. This peace, like a divine ornament, adorns me even today. My friends, envious of my calm demeanor, often questioned, "How do you possess such serenity? Even with all our wealth and riches, we cannot find this peace."

I would reply, "Is there a greater wealth than a mother's love? Seek solace in your mother, for no treasure surpasses her." Hearing this, they would nod in admiration.

Yet, a hidden sorrow lingers within me, haunting me to this day. Throughout my life, I've made countless requests of you, Mother, and you fulfilled each one with a smile. No matter how grand my wishes, they were always small in your eyes. To give me a beautiful world, you sacrificed your own comforts and joys. You, my Mother, the most selfless being, adorned only by the faint traces of a smile—this is your unmatched wealth.

And here I stand, your child, the poorest of the rich, unable to ask you, "What do *you* want, Mother?" This question, unspoken, weighs on me like a burden I cannot lift.

My greatest wish has always been to see you smile wholeheartedly. Yet, I know this remains incomplete. To truly understand you, I must become one with you. But how can I, tied down by the chains of selfish desires, the tangled web of material and worldly bonds? Unlike you, who severed every tie to nurture me selflessly, I remain a mere ordinary being, bound and struggling in the snare of ego and self-interest.

This selfish cage, Mother, is of my own making. This flawed nature, my own doing. And because of this, no matter how high I rise in life, I remain but a mere ant before your towering greatness.

You, who gave everything for my joy, deserve a happiness I could never fully give back. For that, I remain forever your fortunate and also unfortunate child.

—·—·—●—·—·—

The Source of Wisdom

Once, I fell in love with a woman. But she said she couldn't love me back—her heart already belonged to someone else. Broken and dejected, I returned home, tears streaming down my face. I sought solace in my mother's embrace, where my despair found a sanctuary. With her ever-so-gentle smile, she wiped my tears away and said, "Despair has no place in your heart, my child. Love is not something to resent. Those who do not love you deserve no hatred. Instead, focus on those who cherish you. They are countless."

Her words were a blessing. I found someone who loved me deeply, a woman who became my life partner.

I devoted my love to her, and she returned it wholeheartedly. Not once did she oppose me, not even in the smallest way. "Why do you always follow my words without question?" I asked her one day.

"There's magic in your words," she replied. "They sound like the strings of a veena to me. Your words guide me, steering the boat of my life. Where did you learn to speak so beautifully?"

Together, we built a life—a garden of love. We tended it with care, watering it with affection. The garden bloomed, bearing the fruits of our love: beautiful children.

We raised them with devotion, cradling them to sleep on our chests, playing games with them on our shoulders. Every step they took was on a path we paved with flowers. We fulfilled their every wish, never letting them feel the pinch of scarcity, shaping them into complete, compassionate beings.

Yet one day, those same children, who had never questioned us, asked, "Where did you acquire such immense richness of the heart? Who gifted you this wealth of wisdom?"

My life has been graced with countless friends, each one a blessing, their love an endless source of joy. I have never hated anyone. Even when I searched my heart for an enemy, I found none. What a reward for a thousand lifetimes of good deeds!

One day, my friends gathered me into a circle. With firm resolve, they demanded, "Tell us the secret behind your words. They pierce like gentle arrows, touching our hearts and binding us with love. Where did you learn this art of speaking?"

Step by step, I had walked through life, reaching many milestones. Everywhere I went, people celebrated me, marveling at my journey.

At a grand gathering, I was honored as a great lover, an ideal husband, a devoted father, and an invaluable friend. They asked me to speak, and I obliged:

"Words are a collection of letters, but letters are divine. Eternal and unperishable, they are the purest flow of truth. Every word we utter originates from our hearts and takes root in the hearts of others. Letters hold no beginning or end—they are eternal. To understand their power is wisdom.

Each word we speak should be measured: Do our words bring joy or sorrow? Do they unite or divide? Are they sparks of destruction or seeds of creation? Do they guide others toward light or push them into darkness? Do they share love or ignite hatred? Do they offer comfort or deepen someone's grief? Wisdom lies in being mindful of this."

When I finished, the hall fell silent. Everyone looked at me, their faces full of anticipation.

"But where did you learn this wisdom? Which book holds this knowledge? Tell us!" they implored.

"I've read the Upanishads, the Bhagavad Gita, the Bible, the Quran, and Buddha's teachings. I've studied the works of many great minds. My words are a reflection of all these texts," I said.

They didn't seem satisfied. "No, you're hiding something. Tell us the true source of your wisdom," they insisted.

Unsure of what to say, I closed my eyes. Time seemed to stand still, and I felt as if I were floating somewhere far away. After an indeterminate pause, two syllables escaped my lips:

"Am…ma." (Mother).

The hall erupted in applause, resounding with the echo of clapping hands. Tears flowed freely down my cheeks. Amidst my silent sobs, Mother's radiant smile appeared in my mind, her presence filling my heart.

Yes, 'Mother' is the word eternal.

Love Overflowing with Compassion

The only being capable of feeling others' joys as her own, their happiness as her bliss, is none other than a mother. A mother's heart defies the constraints of age, brimming with eternal youth and freshness, like a tender new leaf exuding fragrance and life.

Mother is an ocean of compassion, a boundless glacier perpetually melting into streams of care. Whenever a heart drowns in an ocean of sorrow, her eyes release streams of tears without hesitation. A mother has no enemies, and even if someone perceives her as one, she willingly shoulders their burdens with grace.

Mother is like a condensed cloud, impartial and ever-giving. She feels the pain of all beings—birds, animals, trees, or humans. How astonishing! Even when stones break apart, her heart trembles. I still recall her words: "How many chisel strikes must a stone endure to transform into a sculpture that brings us joy?"

One day, I saw a bird feeding its chicks in a nest carefully woven among tree branches. The sight reminded me of my childhood, when my mother would lovingly feed me morsels of food with her tender hands. I called her over to witness the scene. "Look how adorable those little chicks are!" I exclaimed, delighted. But as I looked at her, I saw her eyes welling up with tears. Puzzled, I asked, "What moved you so much, Mother?" Her gaze remained fixed on the mother bird. "Imagine the lengths to which that mother bird must go, searching far and wide to bring food for her hungry chicks," she said. It was then I understood the depth of her compassion. Such profound empathy—this is what it means to be a mother!

In our backyard, a cow gave birth to a calf. We were all captivated by the sight of the newborn calf—its innocent eyes and tender form melted our hearts. Watching it stumble and struggle to stand, and then run eagerly toward its mother for milk, felt like witnessing a miracle. In my excitement, I clapped and turned to look at my mother.

There she was, embracing the cow with love, stroking its belly with compassion, wiping her tears, and silently listening to the unspoken emotions of the mother cow. Such profound tenderness.

"Do not pluck flowers," she often said. "They are the ornaments of the plants. They belong to the plants, not us. Only offer flowers that have fallen to the ground to the divine—that is true devotion."

"When we feel hungry," she would continue, "trees willingly offer us their fruits. Do not harm them by striking them with stones. Even if they don't bleed red, they bleed all the same."

Oh, Mother, your heart is softer than the petals of a flower and sweeter than the nectar of fruits. From you, I learned compassion. From you, I learned love. I have tried to walk your path, to make my heart like yours. I aspired to be a mother to the world—to love many, to ease the pain of countless souls, and to experience the ultimate joy of giving.

May the compassion and love you instilled in me remain alive forever. Like a river flowing tirelessly, I wish to quench the thirst of all who come my way, ultimately returning to your feet, O ocean of compassion, to bow in gratitude. That is my only wish.

—·—·—●—·—·—

Beauty is Bliss

A rainbow arched across the sky, radiating its seven vibrant colors. My mother sat beside me, urging me to marvel at its splendor. Truly, it adorned the heavens with such elegance, delighting the eyes that beheld it. Yet, within me arose a philosophical question: "Mother, what is the point of admiring such fleeting beauty? Show me something that bestows eternal joy."

"Did you see the rainbow?" she asked.

"Yes, I saw it," I replied.

"Did it bring you joy?"

"Yes, but it's fleeting, Mother."

"Don't merely glance at it and move on, my child. Learn to truly behold it. Nature is a great teacher. Sometimes, it conveys profound lessons in a single moment. At other times, it stays with us as a guiding force, teaching us throughout life. The lessons of nature lay the foundation for lasting joy. Simply observing isn't enough; only when you truly perceive can it leave an imprint on your soul, transforming into wisdom.

The rainbow you dismissed as transient reminds us of the fleeting nature of life itself. It declares a bittersweet truth: we are not eternal. But within its fleeting beauty lies a profound message—if you grasp this truth, you can mold your life into something beautiful, spreading joy to others and moving closer to lasting bliss. The more happiness you spread, the stronger your own joy becomes, eventually reaching a timeless state."

"But, Mother, how can joy be eternal if life itself is impermanent?"

"Even as you live, that joy will journey with you, filling your heart. It will illuminate the lives of those around you, spreading like the rays of the sun. After your time on earth ends, your joy will continue to touch lives—those you know and even those you don't. Like Krishna's flute, Jesus' compassion, Allah's infinite love, or Buddha's serenity, your joy will resonate across generations, shining on eternally."

"How can one attain such joy?" I asked.

"Giving is joy. Sharing love is joy. Living for others is joy. Sacrifice, without expecting rewards, is joy. Spreading knowledge is joy. To live on, even after death, is the greatest joy. These together form eternal bliss. Like the rainbow you saw, such joy radiates in many hues, boundless and immortal like the universe itself."

"You are enough for me, Mother. You are my guide. I don't need anyone else," I said.

"No, my child," she replied. "No single individual can suffice. Accept the universe as your teacher. Keep learning. The one who claims to know it all is ignorant. The one who admits to learning every day is wise. Knowledge is like nectar—the more you taste, the more you desire.

Every being you encounter—be it an insect, an animal, or a fellow human—has something to teach you. Some, with their virtue and growth, will inspire you to follow their path. Others, with their struggles and decline, will warn you away from theirs. Books are not your only teachers; your very life is a school.

The sun is setting now, my child. Let's head home."

That night, I resolved to perceive everything deeply, to embrace and learn from life as my mother had guided me. I fell asleep, grateful to be born human.

In my dream, my mother appeared as a magnificent figure, as vast as a mountain. Rainbows encircled her, hundreds of them. Her face radiated the brilliance of a thousand suns, while her smile cascaded the cool light of a moonlit night. On her forehead danced the wisdom of countless divine scriptures, shimmering like waves of enlightenment.

The universe itself had transformed into my mother—a celestial teacher, an eternal light, turning my dream into a divine reality.

———•———

Milk of Compassion

Throughout my journey, I traveled down countless paths, encountering a myriad of people. Their stories, woven from diverse threads of life, gradually revealed a singular essence—the truth of compassion and sacrifice.

A frail twelve-year-old girl dragged her weary body along the dusty road, her emaciated frame trembling under the weight of her plight. Despite her own hunger, she clutched a piece of bread, a treasure won after relentless effort. I followed her, curious about her resolve. She stopped under a tree where her ailing mother lay, barely alive. With tender care, she fed her mother, her eyes brimming with love and determination.

"Why didn't you eat first?" I asked.

"She is my mother. She gave me life. Without her, I wouldn't exist. Without me, she wouldn't survive," the girl replied before darting off to earn another morsel.

On another day, rain lashed mercilessly as I sought shelter beneath a tree. Beside me stood an elderly man, his frail figure trembling in the storm. Suddenly, a gust of wind swept through, and I stumbled, nearly falling. When I regained my balance, the old man was gone.

Panic-stricken, I searched for him. To my astonishment, he was climbing the tree, his trembling hands reaching out to rescue a tiny bird whose feathers had snagged on a branch. Gently, he freed the creature and returned it to its nest, shielding it from the rain.

"Why take such a risk for a bird?" I questioned, bewildered.

"It has life, too. It deserves protection. That bird has little ones who depend on it," he said, smiling. "Didn't you see its gratitude? It nuzzled my hand before flying back to its nest."

A flash of lightning illuminated the sky, mirroring the glow of fulfillment on the old man's face.

As I journeyed further, I saw blind parents led by their child, their fragile hands clutching hers with unwavering trust. I witnessed a young man carrying his legless mother on his back, showing her the world she had dreamed of. A mother, shielding her daughter's dignity with her tattered sari, walked forward undeterred by the judgmental eyes of strangers.

Everywhere I turned, these profound acts of love and sacrifice filled me with a sense of wonder. The essence of all these moments was clear: *Mothers sacrificing for their children's happiness, and children dedicating their lives to their mothers' well-being.*

Moved by these revelations, I gathered these extraordinary souls and asked, "What is the source of your greatness?"

With one voice, they answered:

"All of this comes from our mothers. Even before we were born, she spoke to us through stories, songs, and whispers, embedding compassion and love into our very being. With her milk, she nourished not only our bodies but our souls, imparting wisdom through every lullaby.

She taught us to spread love, shower kindness, embrace sacrifice, and forge friendships. She instilled in us an endless wellspring of joy. These are the treasures she gifted us, treasures we now share with the world."

Tears welled up in my eyes. The world before me transformed, blooming with newfound beauty, painted by the boundless love of mothers and the compassionate children they nurture.

The Eternal Beauty of Transformation

One evening, my friend and I set out on a walk, heading towards a place he often spoke about. After a while, we stopped before a picturesque house that looked like a serene cottage. My friend led me inside, directing me to rest in a spacious room while he ventured further in.

As I waited, I noticed the ambiance was peculiar. The air was filled with the fragrance of flowers and aromatic incense. The walls were adorned with sensuous paintings, and the laughter of women echoed from within. Gradually, I realized I was in a brothel.

Embarrassed, I rose to leave, but a gentle hand pressed my shoulder, urging me to stay. A strikingly beautiful woman sat beside me, engaging in polite conversation. She attempted to captivate me with her charm and allure, but I remained unmoved.

"You are no ordinary man in disguise, are you?" she teased, trying to provoke me.

"I see you as a fleeting streak of lightning," I replied. "But tell me, will this radiance remain forever? Will these flowers never wither, your beauty never fade, and your youth never wane? Can you promise to stay untarnished, untouched by the stains of the world? Would you accept me not as a patron who degrades, but as an eternal lover who uplifts? Can you offer love without pretense?"

Her response came reluctantly. "This is my profession, my nature. My life is about giving pleasure and finding pleasure in return. My daily routine is to sell my beauty to bring joy to others." With that, she rose to leave.

I gently held her hand and made her sit down. "How long will this theatrical life continue? When your youth fades and your profession ceases, who will stay by your side? Who will stand as your shadow in the end? Embrace true love and experience everlasting joy."

Unimpressed, she retreated into the house, leaving me to wait for my friend. Moments later, her voice resonated from behind the door, soft but curious.

"Where does true, eternal happiness lie?"

"You have a heart, don't you?" I said. "Awaken it. Become a wife to someone who deserves your love. Surrender your heart to him, offer him true love, and bear his children. When you experience the joy of motherhood, eternal happiness will be yours. It will stay with you always."

She walked away, her steps heavy, and I left shortly after.

Later that night, as I served my mother, someone knocked on my door. Opening it, I found the same woman standing there. "I have thought about your words," she said. "They resonate with me. Will you marry me? Will you make me a mother? Will you grant me the experience of motherhood you spoke of? I surrender my heart to you. Will you accept it?"

I helped her rise and took her to my mother. I explained everything, and my mother, understanding my intentions, blessed me. She embraced the woman and welcomed her into our family.

In time, she became my wife and blessed me with children. The joy of nurturing our family transformed her. She abandoned her past roles and embraced a new life with unmatched enthusiasm. Her beauty became timeless, glowing with the love and purity of her new role.

Together, we created a new world. She walked beside me every step of the way, offering support, guidance, and companionship. She anticipated my needs, filled my life with joy, and gave my existence purpose.

One day, she knelt at my mother's feet, tearfully expressing her gratitude. "Like your son, I will raise my children with love and care. Becoming a mother has shown me the greatness of your heart. From a discarded flower, you gave me a place in your heart and life. You taught me the meaning of motherhood and made it a reality. My beauty now is eternal, my joy everlasting, for motherhood is the only truth."

With tears of gratitude, she bathed my mother's feet, sealing the moment with reverence and love.

The Most Beautiful Color

One evening, a renowned Swamiji sat by a riverside, delivering profound teachings. Drawn by his reputation as a treasure trove of wisdom, I decided to attend. Hundreds were seated before him, listening intently as he spoke, weaving insights from scriptures and life experiences into his discourse.

Toward the end, he posed three questions to the audience:

"How many among you consider yourselves ignorant? Raise your hands."

there was Silence. No one moved. Acknowledging ignorance publicly was a step no one was willing to take.

"Fine. How many of you consider yourselves wise?" he asked.

Again, there was no response. People exchanged uneasy glances, hesitant to declare themselves wise.

"So, you're all caught in the liminal space between ignorance and wisdom, like innocent wanderers," he remarked, smiling.

"Now, let me ask a simpler question. Tell me your favorite colors."

The audience came alive, each person enthusiastically naming their favorite color. Beautiful hues of the world spilled out as they voiced their preferences. Then Swamiji declared, "My favorite color is black. To me, it is the most beautiful color of all."

The crowd burst into laughter.

The laughter baffled me. I couldn't discern if it came from the wise or the ignorant among them. I, too, failed to grasp the essence of Swamiji's statement, given my young age.

A skeptical elder voiced his discontent:

"Black? It's darkness, ignorance, despair. What beauty lies in black? Isn't it absurd? Smear coal on a pristine white wall, and it becomes unsightly. If you like black so much, paint your face with it and parade through the streets!"

Without reacting to the remark, Swamiji said, "That's all for today," and retreated behind the curtain.

The audience dispersed in quiet contemplation, as if groping through a fog. I returned home, equally puzzled.

When I arrived, my mother asked, "What did you learn today?"

I tried to recount Swamiji's teachings and ended with the moment he made everyone laugh.

"Great souls speak in layers of meaning, my dear. We must strive to uncover the essence of their words," she said.

I was too young to decipher the subtleties of his message, so I sought my mother's wisdom. I found her meditating peacefully in the garden. Sitting quietly beside her, I watched.

In that moment, she appeared divine—a yogini radiating calm. Her serene face resembled a blooming lotus, while her black tresses danced gently in the breeze. They framed her forehead like the strokes of an artist's brush, accentuating the elegance of her visage.

Her long plait cascaded down her back, a masterpiece of intricate craftsmanship. It seemed alive, like a poised black serpent, exuding strength and grace.

In her flowing black hair, I saw beauty beyond compare—a metaphor for life's complexities. Her locks, interwoven with strands of wisdom and ignorance, mirrored the harmony of human dualities.

They weren't just a mark of physical beauty; they symbolized the journey from darkness to light, ignorance to understanding.

I realized Swamiji's truth in that instant. Black, often misunderstood, is the color of creation, the beginning of wisdom. It absorbs all, shelters all, and holds within it the promise of transformation.

I bowed before my mother, enlightened by the profound lesson she embodied. The beauty of black had unveiled itself through her, a living testament to Swamiji's words.

Eyes Filled with Love

Throughout my journey, I wandered across many lands, meeting countless people and parting ways just as often. As a child, my mother had said, "A person with complete faith looks directly into the eyes of others while speaking."

I began observing everyone I met, scrutinizing their eyes. Yet, none reflected purity or sincerity. They were eyes clouded with flaws—veiled by lust, anger, greed, attachment, pride, or jealousy.

Eyes filled with desires, longing to possess something, always wishing for more. Eyes that only knew how to take but never to give. Eyes burning with envy when denied their desires, radiating sparks of frustration instead of light.

Rajas-filled eyes, restless with anger, incapable of peace. Eyes that could incinerate others with their fiery gaze. Terrifying eyes that suppressed love and spread the flames of hatred like lava across the world.

Eyes that hoarded wealth, possessions, and power, knowing full well they wouldn't carry any of it on their solitary journey after death. Eyes blind to generosity, fixated only on acquiring.

Eyes blinded by greed for wealth, racing after fleeting power, and yet clouded with delusion. Eyes intoxicated by their successes, unable to see clearly, burning with arrogance and diminishing human values in their blindness.

Eyes that refused to make space for love, closing off compassion, devoid of peace, filled with selfish ambition. Eyes that shunned unity and sought to trample others to rise higher, consumed by envy, turning themselves to ashes.

I grew weary of encountering such eyes. Then, I reached a city of bliss—a city of mothers. Everywhere, there were radiant women embodying the sweetness of motherhood. Their youthful glow emanated from the eternal fountain of maternal love.

Their eyes turned toward me, and the light of a million stars reflected upon my face. My exhaustion vanished, and I felt revitalized as if I had been reborn. I flitted among them like a bee, basking in their love-filled gazes, savoring the nectar of their compassion.

These were eyes that never rested, always moving, always alert with concern for their children's well-being. Eyes that woke at dawn, brimming with tenderness, blossoming like flowers to shower love upon their children. Eyes that danced with joy, encouraging their children's laughter and delight.

Eyes hidden beneath graceful lashes, brimming with the tides of compassion, rising and falling like waves in an ocean of care. Eyes that shone like pure, glistening snow, cooling even the sunlit day with their soothing light. Eyes that fulfilled wishes without being asked, sparkling like magical gems.

Eyes that detected their children's struggles even before they could speak of them, cutting through obstacles with sharp resolve. Such were the eyes of mothers, filled with unconditional love.

The eyes of those who strayed from their mothers, chasing after illusions, were the only eyes that seemed dim and hollow.

What a beautiful world it would be if everyone embodied a mother's love! To see through a mother's eyes is to look beyond the surface, to see not just faces but hearts.

Yes, that is what happened to me.

I began looking at the world through eyes of love. Those unworthy of being seen averted their gaze. Those deserving came forward.

I saw eyes filled with helplessness, longing for solace. Eyes weary with hunger. Eyes silently pleading for compassion. Eyes soaked in tears, seeking mercy. Eyes yearning for love.

I saw eyes that revealed the meaning of my existence, calling me toward them. Without hesitation, I took a step forward toward that direction, answering their silent plea.

The Dance of the Little One

An extraordinary display of art was unfolding, one so rare and mesmerizing that I had never experienced anything like it before. I was honored by my friends with a front-row seat, granting me the privilege of witnessing the marvel up close.

Artists showcased their brilliant paintings, filling the room with awe as their creations seemed to reflect new moonrises in our eyes. Dancers performed various intricate styles, their movements captivating us and eliciting thunderous applause. Musicians united, weaving melodies so sweet and soulful that they swayed our hearts and compelled us to nod along in bliss.

Countless other art forms graced the stage that evening, immersing us in a realm of aesthetic ecstasy. The performance continued late into the night, leaving us fulfilled and enchanted as we returned home.

On my way back, memories of the evening intertwined with a scene from my childhood that my father often spoke of—a cherished, heartwarming moment. It was as though the recollection held my hand and led me into the past.

A similar grand spectacle had once taken place in our village. The news of such an illustrious event spread quickly, drawing everyone, young and old, to the venue. My father, being a respected elder, received a special invitation, and artists themselves came to our home to request his presence, asking him to attend with my mother.

The curtain rose, signaling the commencement of the program. Artists gazed upon the packed audience, their satisfaction visible. Yet, to everyone's surprise, the seat next to my father, reserved for my mother, remained empty. Puzzled and concerned, the artists turned to my father.

"She won't come; she declined," my father explained calmly.

The response stirred murmurs of discontent among the artists. Some viewed it as arrogance, others as an insult, while a few speculated about her health. A sense of unease clouded the air, and the artists completed their performance with heavy hearts.

The audience's applause could not reach them; the praise felt hollow. The joy that usually sparkled in their eyes after a successful performance was replaced with redness from unspoken pain. Their minds churned with questions: "Why did she reject our invitation? Is it pride? Or indifference to art?"

Determined to find answers, the artists collectively decided to visit our home. They approached in a group, as if staging a confrontation, their emotions tightly wound.

As they neared our house, they were struck by its glow, the lights radiating like the beams of many moons. Mesmerized, they peered inside quietly.

There, they saw my mother playing with me, her two-year-old child. She sparkled with a divine radiance, entirely immersed in my innocent joy. She listened intently to the tiny sounds I made, savoring the melodies hidden in my babbles. She watched the twinkle in my eyes, marveling at the stars reflected in them. She lifted me gently into the air, delighting in the fluttering movements of my tiny hands as though they were performing an intricate dance.

She hugged me close, as if cradling a masterpiece, and swayed with pure bliss. Then, noticing the artists, she invited them in with a radiant smile.

Humbled by her presence, they sat on the floor in silence, gazing at her with reverence.

"Look at my child," she began. "Can any artist create a masterpiece as wondrous as this? Who can replicate the symphonies in these little sounds? Which dancer can rival the grace of this child's movements? Is there any joy greater than the one a mother feels as she watches her child grow? Can anyone gift a more beautiful world than the one a mother sees in her child's laughter and love?

"Can you capture the cuckoo's song, the ripples of a stream, or the shimmer of waves? My child does all this for me. He dances to the rhythm of my heart and shares every moment with me, gifting me endless springs of joy."

With that, her attention returned to me. She resumed playing, her world complete in the delight of our bond.

The artists sat silently for a long time. Eventually, one whispered, "Perhaps my mother once played with me like this." Another echoed, "Maybe all mothers are the same."

Nodding in agreement, they quietly departed, each retreating to their own thoughts and reflections.

—·—·—●—·—·—

Motherly Love

Early in the morning, there was a knock at the door. I opened it to find a strikingly beautiful woman standing there, her radiance akin to a delicate vine swaying in the breeze. Handing me a soft green letter, as delicate as a tender betel leaf, she spoke, her voice as melodious as the strings of a veena.

"It's a love letter," she said, her words lingering like the softest echo. "I'll wait for your response," she added, her movements as graceful as a lightning streak curling into the horizon.

I opened the letter, and within it lay her heart, unfurled. Delving into its depths, I saw her pain vividly. The scorching heat of summer was burning her, she said, and only the coolness of my gaze could soothe her. The arrows of Cupid's rain had wounded her soul, and she longed for my presence to shield her. She yearned for the warmth of my breath to comfort her through the icy whispers of winter. Above all, she hoped I would fill her life with the light of spring and bring joy to her heart.

I took the letter to my room to place it among my possessions, but was greeted by the rustling whispers of hundreds of letters stored there, fluttering as if to demand, *"What about us?"*

I could do little but add her letter to the growing pile, overwhelmed by the voices of love surrounding me.

How could I respond to all of them? Each writer was beautiful, but what about their hearts? Did their beauty reflect the purity of their souls? Were their intentions grounded in love for *me* as a person or merely for the surface? Questions swirled in my mind, leaving me restless. The letters continued to flutter, demanding, *"Answer us!"*

Unable to bear it any longer, I fled outside, but the letters followed me, surrounding me like a storm of unspoken desires. The letters transformed in to angelic beauties and started chasing me.

"Do you truly love me?" I asked.

A collective murmur responded, "Yes."

"Have you looked into the depths of my heart?"

"Yes," they echoed.

I paused, gathering my thoughts. "I will give away all my wealth and possessions to the poor, keeping nothing for myself. I will stand alone and begin a new life. If anyone wishes to walk this path with me, come."

A few stopped in their tracks.

"I will destroy my vehicles and travel only on foot. If anyone is willing to join me on this journey, come."

A few more paused.

"I will return home each evening, exhausted and hungry. Not just for physical intimacy but for someone to ease my hunger and offer me rest in their embrace. If anyone can do this, come."

More fell behind.

"My path will not be illuminated with moonlight but filled with shadows. If you can scatter light and share my burdens without faltering, come."

When I looked back, no one remained. The crowd stood at a distance, their brows furrowed, hands on their hips, gazing at me with eyes ablaze with anger.

They felt insulted, as if I had dismissed their affection. Together, they shouted at me:

"This isn't love! Love is being drawn to one another, merging into each other's existence. It's about passion, intimacy, and consuming desire. How can you, a clueless fool, speak of love? Are you even a man? While we're drawn to you with longing, you speak like a beggar! You act like an old man in his sixties while still in your twenties. Did you think we were lustful demons to fall for a pauper like you?"

Their words, sharp as arrows, sought to wound me.

"Yes," I replied calmly. "I am a beggar. A beggar who dreams of a perfect woman to share my life. My mother gave me countless blessings, raised me with care, and taught me values. Yet, there are blessings even she couldn't give me—blessings I seek from a woman who can truly love.

"I seek a woman who loves not with her eyes but with her heart. A woman who serves with selflessness, like a mother. Someone who will stand by me in times of hardship, give me courage, and guide me with affection. I want a woman who can see beyond my wealth and understand my hunger.

"I need someone who forgives my flaws and showers me with compassion. My mother filled my life with sweetness; I seek a partner who can add flavor to my existence, someone who can become the nectar of my life.

"I will honor her, cherish her, and place her on a throne in my heart as a queen. I will be loyal to her, and her alone.

"If there is a woman who can love me as a mother loves her child, who can walk beside me on this path of life, I am here, waiting for her. My heart remains open, filled with hope."

I walked forward, leaving them behind. They grew smaller in the distance as I journeyed alone, still searching for the love that mirrored a mother's.

Revelations of the Posture

"Have you heard about it?" my close friend asked excitedly.

"Heard about what?" I replied, puzzled.

"A grand gathering of astrologers is happening nearby. Experts in astrology, palmistry, and numerology from all over have assembled. They can predict your future just by observing how you walk, your facial expressions, or even the letters in your name. I have a special invitation to meet them. Come with me!" he urged.

"But how can they determine our future? Isn't it up to us to shape our destiny?" I asked skeptically.

"I understand your doubts, but let's go. You'll see for yourself," he insisted, dragging me along.

When we arrived, the place was teeming with people. "Are all these people so uncertain about their future that they are ready to follow someone else's direction?" I thought, my curiosity piqued. Thanks to my friend's connections, we were ushered straight to the front of the queue.

The astrologers examined my friend in every possible way—reading his palm, studying his facial expressions, analyzing the letters of his name, and even asking about his birth date. Each offered a different prediction and suggested several paths for his future.

Confused, my friend asked, "Which is the best path for me?"

Instead of answering, the astrologers argued among themselves, each claiming their suggestion was superior. Finally, they concluded, "The choice is yours; all paths are good." This left my friend more uncertain than before.

Next, they turned to me. "Let us tell you your future," they said.

"No, thank you," I replied. "I will carve my own path."

My response enraged them. Feeling insulted, they surrounded me. "How dare you disregard us? We won't let you leave until you show us your horoscope and let us determine your future," they declared.

It took all my effort to escape their grasp. But they weren't done with me—they left the gathering and began chasing me down the street. "Where do you think you're going?" they shouted, running after me.

Desperate, I ran toward the one person who could protect me: my mother. Reaching her, I cried out, "Mother! Mother!"

My mother stepped forward, a shield of calm and strength. She stood between me and the enraged astrologers, her presence commanding silence.

They stopped in their tracks, stunned by her serenity. Words failed them as they stood there, gazing at her face. A profound silence enveloped the scene. The only sound was my labored breathing as I caught my breath.

My mother, her hand firmly on my shoulder, smiled softly at the crowd. Her peaceful gaze and unwavering composure held them spellbound.

"Look at her posture," someone murmured. "How it radiates light! There's not a trace of worry or malice. I've never seen such a divine expression before."

"Notice the vastness of her forehead—it's like the expansive sky. Her round eyes shine like the sun and moon. Her eyebrows arc gracefully, like rainbows. See how her dark, soft hair dances lightly on her forehead, as if performing a tender dance."

"What a marvel! Her face gleams like a lotus in full bloom. Such courage, such contentment, and such unshakable joy—her face is a treasure trove of emotions."

"Her child's future is etched in her forehead. His destiny lies in her eyes. Look at her hands, holding him so firmly yet lovingly. They are a fortress of strength for him."

"Observe how she stands, unwavering. Doesn't it feel like she's laying a foundation for her child's future right here?"

"Yes, with a mother like her, what need is there for horoscopes, numerology, or palmistry? A mother alone can shape her child's destiny."

"Those who rely on their mothers are truly blessed. Compared to her, what do our so-called sciences amount to?"

One by one, the astrologers fell silent. Then, turning to each other, they said, "We've been chasing this boy, seeking to predict his future, but he has shown us the truth. His mother is his destiny, his foundation. Today, we've witnessed the ultimate truth. Let us return to our own mothers and seek solace in their love."

With that, they departed, leaving me alone with my mother. She pulled me close, her embrace radiating the same unshakable love and protection that had silenced the crowd. Resting my head on her shoulder, I felt an indescribable peace, as if the entire universe had been reduced to the gentle, comforting rhythm of her heart.

—·—·—●—·—·—

The Leading Light

My journey through life has been filled with countless experiences, each offering new lessons and enriching my understanding. As a perpetual student, every step forward has expanded my knowledge and shaped my perspective. The world itself has been my teacher, revealing truths and showing me the roots of wisdom.

One day, I was sitting alone in our flower garden, marveling at nature's beauty and the divine craftsmanship behind it. Suddenly, a bird fell from a tree branch to the ground. I rushed to it, gently picking it up and comforting it. The bird looked at me with gratitude, its injured state stirring my heart. Tears flowed freely as I witnessed its vulnerability. After a moment of rest, the bird regained strength, fluttered its wings, and soared back into the sky.

Why did my heart react so strongly? What moved me to act without hesitation? What unseen force melted my otherwise resolute self? Was this the essence of compassion? Was this what is often referred to as divine grace? Who had gifted me this capacity for such deep empathy? I didn't have the answers, but this encounter brought me face to face with a new, profound part of myself.

Reflecting on this experience, I pressed forward, encountering many more moments that clarified the essence of life. Just as the world is essential for human existence, every life event is crucial for personal growth. The world is a boundless school, its lessons far surpassing those found in textbooks. Here, there are no exams to pass, only an endless curriculum to absorb until our last breath.

Until now, my life has been a fulfilling and joyous journey. I've been able to lend a helping hand to those in need, feed the hungry, and guide my peers toward righteousness. With courage as my breath, I've stood against injustice and hoisted the flag of truth to the skies. My heart, overflowing with love, has shared its nectar with everyone I've met, receiving love in return. I've thrived as a human being, filled with humanity, creating an inner garden of eternal spring where I could leap, dance, and revel in boundless joy.

Evil forces—dishonesty, cruelty, envy, and hatred—have tried countless times to conquer me, to turn me into something monstrous. They've attacked in various guises, but their attempts have always ended in failure. Even now, they try to creep in, only to collapse powerless before they can reach me.

One day, a question arose in my mind: How have I been able to repel such powerful adversaries? Where did this inner strength come from? No one explicitly taught me this resilience. Could it be my own greatness? Who planted this seed of discernment within me, nurturing it into a mighty tree? Who could it be?

I pondered and pondered, until weariness closed my eyes. In that moment, my mother's image appeared before me. With her lustrous black hair and radiant face, she looked as beautiful as a full moon from my childhood memories. Smiling softly, she gazed at me.

Her hair, parted neatly in two, framed her face just as it had when I was a child. She wore her hair in a thin, elegant plait, and I remembered asking her countless times why she styled it that way. "Why not tie it like others do?" I would plead, but she would dismiss my requests with her gentle smile.

Her parting extended gracefully, like a golden thread amidst her dark locks, stopping at a single point on her forehead—a radiant center.

Gradually, the fog of my ignorance lifted, and the dawn of realization broke. The truth became clear, dissolving the clouds of doubt.

My mother's parting symbolized the path she laid for me, separating truth from falsehood, righteousness from unrighteousness, justice from injustice, compassion from cruelty, selflessness from selfishness, and love from hatred. Her parting stretched forward, laying a trail of flowers that led to a singular point: the boundless bliss of life's ultimate truth.

Though the world offers countless teachers, my mother has been my first and greatest guide. From my earliest days, she taught me the distinction between knowledge and ignorance without uttering a word. Step by step, she showed me that life, when approached with wisdom and discernment, can lead to infinite joy. She is the extraordinary being who gifted me this understanding, my eternal Guru—my mother.

Reflections of Beauty

The sky was veiled with clouds. Dark clouds drifted as if herds of cranes were soaring across the heavens. Whispering to the earth they adored, the clouds danced to the tunes of the wind. Gradually, the breeze gained strength. While standing outside, savoring the coolness, I retreated to my room and sat down. Gentle gusts swept through the room, playfully caressing me.

In the corner, a bundle of love letters caught my eye. These were sent by many admirers, penned with tender hearts and delicate hands. The breeze made them flutter, drawing my attention. Buoyed by the refreshing weather, my mind danced in joy. I gathered the letters, held them close, and began reading them one by one.

I had read these letters countless times before. Yet, each reading felt new, as if they were imbued with a timeless charm. Stories of beauty and poetry described in these letters reminded me of poets who had immortalized grace and allure in their verses. I was enamored by how these admirers had poetically described me.

There were those who longed to play with my hair, swaying in the breeze. Some dreamed of gazing at their reflections in my eyes, while others yearned to place their lips on mine and savor the nectar of love. Some wished to lay their heads on my chest, listening to the rhythm of my heartbeat as if it were music. Others desired to hold my waist firmly, feeling victorious in their embrace. There were also those who wanted to walk beside me, step by step, until the end of time.

I stood before the mirror, looking at my reflection. It dawned on me that these admirers weren't exaggerating. In fact, my beauty seemed even greater than their words described. Filled with pride,

I admired myself. The confidence of a heroic prince surged within me. I believed that the great poetic heroes described in epics should bow before me. No wonder so many admirers pursued me, shedding their inhibitions and baring their hearts. "Yes, I am the embodiment of love's charm," I thought, and with this elation, I lay down to sleep. The breeze from outside lulled me into slumber, and I dreamed sweet dreams throughout the night.

The sun rose, its warm rays waking me. I glanced out the window. The sky was clear. "Where have the clouds gone? The ones that entertained me all night? And the soothing breeze—where has it disappeared?" I wondered. My gaze fell upon the love letters, all still in place.

I got up and stood before the mirror again, basking in my beauty. I kissed my reflection and stood tall with my hands on my waist. Adjusting my well-groomed moustache, I admired myself for a while. Unable to tear myself away from the mirror, I preened further and finally stepped outside with the pride of a bumblebee.

In our yard, a gathering of women was chatting animatedly. Among them sat my mother, serene and radiant like a lotus blooming in a tranquil lake. Gradually, their focus shifted from mundane topics to admiring my mother. Listening to their praise filled me with joy.

"Her jet-black hair, her crescent-shaped brows, her luminous eyes—she's a vision of perfection," they declared. They described her with such precision and adoration that they concluded, "Our village has no one as beautiful as her."

My mother gently turned her head and said, "The beauty you see in me pales compared to the beauty of my child. Go home and look at your children—you'll find their beauty surpasses your own."

Her words filled me with pride and a hint of embarrassment. My belief in my own beauty swelled. Yet, one of the women countered, "You may say that, but isn't every part of your child's beauty a reflection of you? Without you, where would your child's charm come from?"

I was struck by their words. Rushing inside, I stood before the mirror. "Am I truly handsome? Is this beauty not my own?" I questioned myself. To my astonishment, my reflection faded, and in its place appeared my mother's face.

I realized the depth of my arrogance. Every ounce of beauty I possessed was but a reflection of hers. "I am a beautiful fool," I confessed to myself.

Overwhelmed by this revelation, I ran to my mother. Standing before her, I was awestruck. I saw myself in her. We were reflections of each other. From that moment on, I began worshipping her beauty and spirit, dedicating myself to her with reverence.

Perhaps that is why, even today, people still see me as handsome—for I am but a reflection of my mother's eternal beauty.

A Ray of Light in the Darkness

It is said that the day and night are equal parts of time. Nature's laws make this true. Yet, in human life, it felt untrue. Life seemed more shrouded in darkness than bathed in light. Aimless exhaustion, unceasing pursuits, and restless hunts for unknown desires characterized the journey. The fleeting joy of a fulfilled dream would soon be overshadowed by new longings, dark clouds of dissatisfaction ever looming.

I didn't want my mother to know of my despair; it would trouble her. Sharing with friends didn't help either—they had their own burdens, often heavier than mine. "Is everyone carrying such unfulfilled dreams?" I wondered. Some had everything yet craved more, while others, having nothing, struggled in silence. When I sought answers, my questions were met with counter-questions about life's purpose, leaving me directionless.

In my confusion, I realized only one sanctuary held answers— my mother's embrace. I turned to her, laying my troubled heart at her feet.

"Why does the garden of life only bloom with black flowers? Everywhere I go, they mock me with their presence. Can't life offer a sunrise of hope, a blossom of joy? Does human existence lack waves of happiness, moments of true peace? Mother, you know everything; guide me!" I pleaded, kneeling before her.

"Walk with me," she said, her voice steady as a flowing river. Holding her hand, I began a journey beside her.

The day was bright, the world radiant with sunlight. People rushed about, chasing their dreams with urgency. The world shone with possibilities. "If only every day were like this," I mused. "Why must there be dark nights?"

We stopped in a garden, vibrant with flowers.

"Shall we rest here?" she asked, and I nodded, sitting beside her.

"Look over there," she said, pointing to a sunflower glowing in the golden sunlight.

"What do you see?"

"It's just a sunflower, as usual. Nothing extraordinary."

"Don't see it as you always have. Look anew."

I stared at the sunflower, watching it turn from east to west, following the sun's path. Yet, it revealed nothing extraordinary to me.

Evening descended, and the sun dipped below the horizon. The moon rose, casting a gentle glow. Nearby, a pond came alive as lotuses bloomed, adorning the water with their beauty.

"Did you see that?" she asked.

"Yes, mother. The lotuses are beautiful. The pond is enchanting. That's what I desire, mother—a life filled with sunlight and moonlit nights, nothing more."

She smiled, holding my hand as she stood. "Let's go home," she said. Her silence puzzled me, but I followed her without question.

Days passed. Though my impatience grew, I trusted her completely. Then, one night, she took me outside into the darkness. Holding my hand, she led me to a place where a sweet fragrance filled the air. Inhaling deeply, I asked, "Where is this divine scent coming from?"

"These are night-blooming flowers, *Rajnigandha*," she said. "They bloom only in darkness, filling the world with their fragrance. They remain unseen yet grace the world with their essence. Their purpose lies in waiting for the night to spread their beauty."

We lingered there for a while before heading home. That night, my mother imparted a profound lesson that illuminated my shadowed life.

"Life is a blend of light and dark. To shine in sunlight is the sun's glory; to glow in moonlight is the moon's splendor. But to illuminate the world with fragrance in utter darkness—that is true greatness. Darkness is the path to light. It is the foundation of truth-seeking. If your life feels enveloped in darkness, it means you are ready to gain wisdom. This vast universe itself is wrapped in darkness, yet the sun and moon navigate it, radiating their light. You must be like them. Even in darkness, bring joy to others.

"Don't be like the sunflower that withers as the sun sets, or the lotus that shrinks as moonlight fades. Be like the *Rajnigandha*, eagerly awaiting the night, thriving in it, spreading beauty and hope. Then, despair will never touch you, and you will stand as a unique light. The sun and moon are within you. Shine from within."

Her wisdom, a treasure trove of all sciences, transformed my life, shaping me into the person I am today—a beacon navigating life's darkness with resilience and purpose.

———•——•—●—•——•———

A Language Beyond Borders

"Mother, I have to leave for a foreign country for a week. I need to settle some business matters. I'll go and return soon," I told her.

"I'll come too. Take me with you," she insisted.

"It's an unfamiliar place, Mother. Even I, fluent in four foreign languages, might struggle there. The people speak only their language and no other. You only know your native tongue. It's better if you don't come," I reasoned.

"I've walked the earth with you all my life. Now, I wish to soar in the skies. Won't you fulfill this wish?" she pleaded. She sounded like a child to me, her innocence disarming. Reluctantly, I agreed. I made all necessary arrangements and brought her along.

As we ascended into the skies, I asked, "It's your first time flying. Aren't you scared?"

"As long as I have your wings to support me, I have no fear," she replied.

When we arrived, we were given a spacious guestroom to stay in. I ensured she was comfortable, explained everything she needed to know, and promised to take her out in the evening to show her the city's beauty. With that, I left for my meeting.

The meeting went well, wrapping up earlier than expected. Eager to explore the city with her, I hurried back to the guestroom. But when I entered, she wasn't there. Panic set in. I searched everywhere, asked everyone, but no one had seen her. Fear gripped me as my mind spiraled into worst-case scenarios.

"Mother! Mother!" I called out desperately, tears blurring my vision. The sun was setting, casting long shadows over my growing dread. I ran through streets and alleys, frantically searching. Finally, I reached a nearby park and saw a group of ten people sitting together, chatting animatedly. To my astonishment, Mother was sitting among them, her face radiating joy.

She wasn't distressed; she seemed at peace. My heart swelled with relief and confusion. How had she managed this? She didn't know their language, nor they hers. Yet they were conversing effortlessly, their bond palpable.

I approached her cautiously. The group greeted me warmly, their expressions welcoming.

"Mother doesn't know your language, and you don't know hers. How are you all communicating? How do you understand each other?" I asked, still perplexed.

One of them smiled and replied, "Her flowing black tresses swaying in the breeze, the graceful arch of her eyebrows, her expressive eyes brimming with love, the playful dance of her lips, and the eloquent gestures of her hands—these spoke volumes to us."

"To connect hearts, who needs words?" Mother interjected. "The sweetness of friendship transcends language."

I stood there, feeling like a child lost among celestial beings. These women seemed like goddesses, not ordinary mortals. Overwhelmed, I held Mother's hand, ready to lead her away.

The group was reluctant to let her go. They watched in silence, their eyes heavy with emotion. "I'll return tomorrow!" she promised. "I cannot stay confined in that glass cage for too long." Her words comforted them, though their tear-filled eyes told a different story.

Walking back with her, I remained awestruck. Their language had been incomprehensible to me, yet they seemed to share a profound connection with her. Perhaps this was a language unique to mothers—a universal tongue only they understood. After all, from the moment a child is born, a mother comprehends their unspoken words. How could any language be foreign to her?

The Natural Symphony

A singing competition was held on a grand stage. Many participated, including me. The winners were announced, but my name wasn't among them. The victors were honored with great applause. The event concluded, the venue emptied, and I left with a heavy heart.

Sitting alone on a large rock, I brooded for a long time, trying to console myself. Yet, the pain didn't subside—not because I didn't win a prize, but because of the humiliation I faced on stage.

The audience had clapped and cheered for my song, appreciating it wholeheartedly. Yet, for some reason, the judges didn't like it. They even seemed angry at the way I sang.

"There's no pitch, no rhythm, no melody, and no proper structure to your song. You can't sing. This should be your last performance. Don't dare step on stage again!" they scolded.

"But my mother loves my singing. She keeps asking me to sing again and again," I responded, trying to defend myself.

My words were met with laughter. "Then sing for your mother's ears alone. Leave now," they dismissed me.

Even those who had clapped for me earlier now looked at me with pity. With a heart heavy with sorrow, I stepped off the stage.

As I was about to leave, an elderly man held my hand and stopped me. "Let's wait and see if they give you a prize. If not, I will give you one myself," he said, making me sit beside him. Despite his reassurance, I left without a prize. He placed some money in my hand, but when I tried to return it, he disappeared into the crowd.

Still burdened by grief, I sat on that rock, unable to move. I felt I couldn't find solace anywhere except in my mother's embrace. I ran home to her.

"Mother! Why did the judges reject the song you love so much? Why was I humiliated in front of everyone when you've always praised my voice? What went wrong, Mother? You never lie, you never give false praise—so why did this happen?" I asked, tears streaming down my face.

She listened to me patiently, a gentle smile on her face. Pulling me close, she comforted me. "Come with me for a while," she said.

We went to a serene pond. It was quiet, save for the rustling of leaves and the occasional chirping of birds. A cuckoo sang from a branch nearby. "Listen carefully," Mother instructed. I closed my eyes and let the melody envelop me. It was soothing, pure, and unbounded.

As the cuckoo flew away, gentle ripples formed on the pond's surface, creating soft gurgling sounds as they lapped the shore. Mother and I sat silently, listening to the natural music of the water.

A bumblebee hummed as it flitted between flowers, its wings creating a rhythmic buzz. We heard a lullaby sung by a mother to her baby in a nearby swing. We listened to a shepherd singing freely in a green meadow, his voice captivating even the cattle.

As we wandered further, we heard a beggar woman singing sorrowfully, her voice heavy with longing. We heard a laborer's melody as he sang to unwind after a long day of hard work. We heard the sweet harmony of a couple, lost in their world of love. We even heard the powerful, defiant chants of workers marching together for their rights.

Everywhere, there was music—a symphony created by life itself. As we returned home, my heart felt lighter, the melodies still resonating in my ears.

"Did you hear it, my child?" Mother asked. "The whole world is filled with music. Who is a greater musician than Nature? If you truly listen, even the smallest creatures and the five elements of Nature sing their songs. The stage where you sang is but a tiny fragment compared to the vastness of this symphony. The music performed there follows rules and restrictions. But the songs you sing on this earth—those are true songs of freedom.

"Don't sing for prizes, my dear. Sing for your soul's contentment. Don't sing for others' approval; sing for your own joy. Judges look for faults in others. But music is a divine gift. It doesn't conform to limits or conditions. Sing freely, sing joyfully, and move forward."

Her words filled me with inspiration. My heart became light, as if I were soaring in the moonlit sky.

"Tired as I am, my child, sing me a song," she requested.

I felt an overwhelming wave of love and gratitude. I began singing for her, and she nodded in delight, her face radiant with happiness. I kept singing, and she kept smiling.

—•—•—●—•—•—

Heart to Heart

A new family moved into our street, hailing from a faraway town. The head of the family was a senior engineer working in the mines. They had a son, our age, who studied in a distant city and visited the village once a week.

Our elders encouraged us to befriend him, saying we could learn many good things and adopt better habits from such a cultured family. Excited by this idea, we eagerly tried to make friends with him.

But the more we tried to get close, the more he distanced himself. He was delicate and reserved, like a freshly bloomed flower. He wore pristine white clothes that resembled jasmine flowers and would avoid us at every chance, mocking us for our lack of education, refinement, and manners. His scornful remarks made us retreat, feeling humiliated.

As time passed, the distance between us grew. Distance turned into dislike, and dislike into envy. We felt someone should teach him a lesson. One evening, united in our resentment, we gathered and decided to confront him.

It was nighttime, and only his room was lit. Our plan was to tease and provoke him. As we reached the window, we peered inside.

He was arguing with his mother, expressing his frustration. He complained about disliking the village, saying it lacked peace and friends. His mother was trying to persuade him otherwise, extolling the purity of village air, water, and hearts. But he dismissed her arguments, belittling us as ignorant, uncultured, and primitive, akin to animals wandering aimlessly.

Hurt by his words, we quietly walked away, each of us burdened by a mix of shame and anger. Back home, my mother noticed my dejected face and asked what had happened. I narrated everything to her in detail.

Mother smiled and said, "You cannot summon a true friendship with mere words. It must come from the heart. Hands can shake, hugs can be exchanged, but for love and friendship, a genuine heart is needed. Not just words, but actions must appeal to others. Approach him again, not with words, but with deeds. Invite him once more; he will surely come."

Her wisdom gave me comfort and strength. I let go of my hurt, and for the first time in days, I slept peacefully.

The next day, we regrouped and visited his home. There he was, sitting alone in his room, wearing the same forlorn look. This time, instead of confronting him, I gently placed a freshly ripened mango on his windowsill, where he could see it. The fragrant aroma filled the air, and we watched from a distance.

He noticed the mango, and his face lit up with joy. Curious, he picked it up, inhaling its sweet scent. He looked out the window to see who had left it, but we had stepped back, pretending to play in the nearby grove.

Soon, he stepped out of his room and followed us into the grove. We continued playing as if unaware of his presence, running, laughing, and enjoying ourselves. Slowly, he began to feel drawn to our games, our laughter, and our camaraderie. Step by step, he came closer, until finally, he joined us.

The boy who once mocked us was now one of us. We played until exhaustion, forgetting even our hunger.

His mother, searching for him, eventually found us in the grove. She was stunned to see her once-isolated son covered in dirt but brimming with happiness. His joy was reflected in her teary eyes.

When she asked him to return home, he refused, saying, "Mother, I love this village. I thought they were just villagers, while I was like a proud flower. But I've realized that a flower cannot bloom without soil. These friends have shown me what true joy is. I want to play, eat, and live with them. Villages are far better than cities, aren't they?"

His words brought a smile to his mother's face as she embraced him. "Every place has its own beauty, my dear. The Creator has gifted us a beautiful world. If we open our hearts and embrace the world around us, every place becomes wonderful. Life's purpose is to live in harmony with everyone—people, animals, birds, and nature all invite us to befriend them. Forget boundaries and walk together; that's the true meaning of life!"

Her words echoed my mother's wisdom. Indeed, all mothers speak the same language of love. From that moment, we all became one, dissolving the barriers of distance and differences, and began a journey of shared joy and togetherness.

The Divine Shrine

From my childhood to this day, I have conversed with countless people, sharing thoughts and emotions. Yet, I have never experienced the sweetness of speaking with anyone else as I have with my mother. In her words, I found joy, comfort, encouragement, purity, and an unparalleled understanding of life. Her presence could turn ages into moments, with a magical touch that transcended everything else.

Mother never adorned herself with ornaments, nor did she ever desire them. Even during festivals and celebrations, she would simply hold my hand and attend the events with me. While other women glittered with their radiant jewels, my mother alone stood out, glowing with pure joy that outshone everyone else.

One day, as we were conversing, I asked her, "Why is this so, Mother?"

She smiled and replied, "As long as I have you, why would I need any ornaments?"

I insisted, "But Mother, ornaments would enhance your beauty!"

Her response was profound, "Ornaments are lifeless creations of humans. You, my dear child, are the divine gift from God who completes my life. Compared to you, all those trinkets are insignificant."

Her words filled my heart with immense happiness.

"When you are near, my body dances like a streak of lightning. My face radiates joy, my eyes shine like the sun and the moon, and my ears sway like flower petals as they listen to your voice. My curls sway playfully as I nod to your words, and my lips quiver with sweetness as they speak to you. When I touch you, my hands feel as if they are caressing a garland of divine flowers. Holding you to my chest, I hear its rhythm blending with the music of my heart. Tell me, my dear, what other adornment could a mother possibly need besides sharing these moments with her child?"

Even today, her words resonate deeply within me, guiding me forward. The parts of her being that I once thought needed adornment became sanctuaries of love, inspiring me and staying with me as my closest companions.

Her curls taught me the joy of playfulness. Her serene face filled me with calmness. Her radiant eyes infused me with confidence. Her words paved flowered paths for my journey. Her voice became the song that lifted me from despair, a perennial wake up song for my soul. Her shoulders cradled me to sleep with lullabies. The rhythm of her heartbeats composed a melody that steered my life. In this way, Mother and I became each other's ornaments, complementing and completing one another.

Above all, her navel became a sacred symbol of protection in my heart, an eternal sanctuary etched into my memory. As a child, whenever fear gripped me, I would run to her, wrap my arms around her waist, and hold on tightly, tears streaming down my face.

In those moments, her navel would touch my cheeks, offering a feeling as if it were wiping away my tears and caressing me with comfort. I would press my face against her navel, feeling an unexplainable sense of safety, as though it were the center of my world.

From the moment I came to life as a tiny being within her womb to my first breath on this earth, her navel was the lifeline that connected us. It nourished me, nurtured me for nine months, and became my first bond with life. When I was born, it gently severed itself, granting me the freedom to breathe and exist independently.

Even today, whenever I see a woman's navel, I regard it as a divine shrine, a sacred emblem of creation, and bow to it in reverence. My mother's navel remains a symbol of pure sanctity, the first bridge of life that connected us and still fills my being with gratitude and awe.

———•———•———●———•———•———

The Eternal Shelter

At forty-two, burdened by the strains of work and the crushing weight of responsibilities, an intense longing surged within me to see my mother. Without delay, I made my way to her.

There she sat in the courtyard, cross-legged in deep meditation, a serene and timeless presence. As I approached, I laid my weary head on her lap. Instantly, the tension in my mind dissolved, and a profound peace enveloped me.

Without opening her eyes, she smiled and said, "So you've come, my dear!"

Surprised, I asked, "How did you know it was me?"

Her reply was as tender as it was profound: "Who else but my child has the privilege to rest his head in my lap? Even God himself would need my permission to touch me—except for you, my child!"

To her, I am, was, and always will be a baby.

In summer, she is the cool shade that quenches my thirst. In winter, she is the warm blanket of love that shields me. In the rain, she offers the edge of her sari as an umbrella, letting herself be soaked in joy. She is an ocean of compassion, sacrificing herself for my comfort.

Countless times, I have found solace in her lap. She has always been my spring, breathing fresh hopes into me when I was parched with despair. She has been my gentle summer breeze, filling my days with vitality. She has been my monsoon rain, infusing me with energy when I faltered. She has been my moonlight, illuminating dark and treacherous paths when fear threatened to overwhelm me.

She has been my relentless summer sun, burning away my doubts and insecurities to make me stronger.

For me, she is a goddess who transcends even divinity itself.

As I rested my head on her lap, she caressed my hair with her soft hands. Though her eyes remained closed, she knew why I had come. She knew everything without me uttering a word. She knew what I needed.

The day passed with me by her side, immersed in her warmth and love. I played in the garden of childhood memories. I relished the sweetness of her love in every morsel she fed me. Her presence healed wounds I didn't even realize I carried.

When evening came, I bid her farewell. I returned home with a heart renewed, the shadows of my troubles lifted.

Strangely, I never told her why I came. She never asked. Yet, without words, she had answered every unspoken question. In her silent way, she had soothed my soul, restored my spirit, and infused me with strength to face the world anew.

Earlier that day, a friend had asked me, "When I'm overwhelmed, I head to the bar. Where do you go?"

"I go to my mother," I had replied.

"You're lucky," he said, his voice tinged with melancholy. "When I was a child, my parents sent me away to a boarding school. By the time I was old enough to return, they had passed on. I never knew what a mother's love felt like. If there's another life, I wish to be reborn as your brother and experience the warmth of your mother's lap."

His words resonated deeply with me. Indeed, there is no greater wealth in this world than a mother's love. It is a treasure beyond compare, a sanctuary that heals, strengthens, and uplifts—a bond that transcends time and space.

The Lightning Memory

I saw a beggar by the roadside. His tattered clothes, disheveled hair, worn-out beard, and frail body epitomized poverty itself.

I asked the driver to stop the car and approached him. Handing over the food I had brought, I felt a sense of satisfaction, a subtle pride in having helped someone in need. But as I was about to leave, he looked at me and smiled. It wasn't a smile of emptiness—it held a mix of many emotions, none of which I could understand.

"Are you leaving, or will you stay and share a meal with me?" he asked.

Caught off guard, his question sent a shiver down my spine. It felt like a sharp jab on my back. I turned to look at him. He didn't seem like a man who had nothing. He appeared like someone who had renounced everything—a sage filled with profound wisdom.

Without saying a word, I sat down beside him on the ground. He took a morsel of food, shaped it, and handed it to me. I ate without hesitation. His expression seemed to hold countless lessons.

"My vehicle is a car; his are his legs. I have a grand entrance; his doorway is the world. My pockets are full of money; his heart is full of peace. I can buy anything in the world, but he can renounce anything that comes his way. I live a life of indulgence; he lives a life of detachment."

He smiled and nodded as if he read my thoughts. Bowing to him in respect, I prepared to leave.

"Can you live like me? Can you step out of the darkness? Then you'll find that life is all light, all brightness," he said.

His words lingered in my mind as the car sped away. My personal secretary, who had witnessed the entire incident, seemed displeased. "I didn't like what you did," he said.

I remained silent for a while, noticing his impatience.

"This reminds me of an incident from my childhood," I began. "It's coming back to me now. Would you like to hear it?"

He nodded.

"When I was about ten years old, my friends and I were playing in an open field. After some time, a boy approached us. He was covered in dirt, wearing tattered clothes, and had no shoes. His mother, a beggar, stood at a distance, watching us with hope as her son asked to join our game.

But we rejected him outright and excluded him. Even as we played, he and his mother watched us from afar, cheering and smiling. She lovingly stroked his head, finding joy in his small happiness.

When the game ended, she approached us and requested that we let her son play with us. Her tone made us uneasy, and we all ran away.

That night, I couldn't shake the image of that mother and her son. As I prepared to sleep, I closed the windows and turned off the lights in my room. Yet through the window, I imagined seeing them at a distance, their eyes pleading. 'Will you be my son's companion?' 'Am I unworthy of your friendship?' they seemed to ask. Fear gripped me, and I ran to my mother, hugging her tightly.

I recounted everything to her. She stroked my back gently and consoled me. 'Don't dwell on it, my child. Always look forward, and that's why God placed your eyes in the front. Light always comes from ahead. If you keep looking back for light, you'll only see your shadow, and it will frighten you. Sleep peacefully; tomorrow will bring light,' she said.

The next morning, my mother asked me to accompany her. 'Where are we going?' I asked. 'To visit an old friend,' she replied. 'It's been years since I've seen her. She'll be happy to see you.'

We walked for a long distance and entered a narrow, cramped neighborhood. The homes there couldn't be called houses—they were dilapidated, lifeless shacks. The people there seemed like mere shadows draped in worn-out clothes. I felt suffocated but followed my mother without protest.

She stopped at a small hut and took me inside. There, I saw a frail woman whose life seemed to be hanging by a thread. Despite her state, she rushed to embrace my mother.

Their hearts met in a profound connection. They hugged and shed silent tears, wiping each other's sorrow away.

The woman spread a torn mat on the ground, and they sat together, conversing without any pretense. Time seemed to pause as they shared their moments. Slowly, understanding began to blossom within me. I learned profound truths about life and realized that love between hearts transcends physical appearances and social barriers.

My mother introduced me to her friend. I walked up to her and hugged her. It felt like I was hugging my mother herself.

As we left, my mother didn't say anything to me. She didn't have to. I had already realized my mistake and resolved to correct myself.

Later that day, my friends and I returned to the field. The beggar woman and her son were waiting for us. I approached them and held the boy's hand, leading him to join us.

Since that day, I've never let go of that hand. He became my companion, my partner, walking beside me in my life's journey.»

Hearing my story, my secretary was moved. "May I ask who that person is now?" he inquired.

The car came to a halt by the roadside. The driver, who had been silent until then, turned to us with a smile. "I am that companion," he said.

The car resumed its journey, picking up speed, moving forward into the light.

The Lesson off the School

A cloud of despair and hopelessness, unlike anything I had ever experienced, loomed over me. The world around me turned gray, mocking my existence. Gentle breezes, once soothing, now agitated me. The songs of birds sounded like irritating cries. Even the moonlight seemed harsh, emitting an unbearable heat. It felt as though the ground beneath me had disappeared, leaving me trapped in a bottomless abyss. How had I become so weak and lost?

I was in my early teens, just sprouting the first traces of maturity. I had stepped into higher education, surrounded by new faces. Childhood had faded into the past, replaced by the first steps of adulthood, burdened with responsibilities and ambitions. It was the first time I had to leave my mother's embrace and navigate a new world alone—a baptism into life's battles, armed only with my courage.

Everyone around me seemed more capable, more intelligent. I felt like an outsider among unfamiliar teachers and peers. For the first time, I was away from home, living in a hostel. That year felt unbearably heavy, an endless struggle to adapt to a world that felt foreign.

I failed my annual exams. It was my first defeat in life, a moment of deep humiliation. I was the only one who failed. People ridiculed me; no one consoled me. Teachers declared me worthless, a failure without a future. Despair weighed heavily on me, suffocating my spirit.

I didn't know what to do. Like a blind man searching for light, I stumbled through my anguish and ran to my mother. I knelt before her, defeated like a soldier who had lost a battle, unable to lift my head.

She reached out and touched me—gently, lovingly, like the soothing light of the moon. Resting my head on her feet, I wept, my tears soaking her feet. She lifted my chin, but I couldn't hold her gaze.

"I failed, Mother. For the first time, I have failed," I said, my words heavy with shame. "I couldn't pass my exams. Everyone says I'm useless."

"You haven't failed, my son," she said, her voice filled with unwavering conviction. "This is not the end but the foundation of your future success. Every stumble is a step toward strength. Rest for now. We will talk later."

Her words were unlike anything I'd ever heard. They were nectar—words only a mother could speak.

She fed me a hearty meal and showered me with unconditional love, waiting patiently until she was sure I had fully recovered.

Then she began to speak, her words stirring my soul and awakening my spirit.

"Birds build their nests with their own skill. They soar on their wings, gathering food each day and resting contentedly on a branch they trust. Fish swim through the waters, performing miraculous dances, living fully in the present moment without worrying about tomorrow. Animals graze to their fill and rest under a tree's shade, living simple, content lives. They don't compare themselves to one another. They live in harmony with their nature. Who taught them these skills, my son?

Classes, divisions, competitions, dominance—these are burdens humanity carries, not the natural world. The desire to surpass others leads to such misery. Did sages like Valmiki or Vyasa attend any school? Who taught wisdom to Christ, or enlightenment to Buddha? Many great scientists, dismissed as failures, conducted experiments that transformed humanity. Didn't the world learn from them?

You are a unique individual. Don't compare yourself to anyone else. Compare yourself only to your past self. Strive to improve. Schools can impart limited knowledge, but the infinite world teaches boundless wisdom. Seek mastery in this vast, limitless school. True education shapes a person, not just their intellect.

The birds, the bees, the trees—they are your teachers. Learn from them. Failing an exam is like stumbling; you can correct it. But don't let life's stumbles go uncorrected, for they are harder to fix."

Her words were like divine teachings, filling me with new vitality. "The lessons learned in a mother's lap surpass those taught in any classroom."

"Mother, are you a psychologist?" I asked, marveling at her wisdom.

"No, my son. I am just a mother, like any other," she replied.

That day, her teachings lifted me from despair and turned me into a relentless seeker of success. Her wisdom became the foundation for my victories, which came in abundance.

Today, I soar in the vast sky like a colorful kite, free and unbound. Yet one truth remains etched in my heart: the string that lets me fly is still held firmly in my mother's hands. That is why her face always radiates joy, glowing with pride in my achievements.

The Divine Manifestation

"There's a sage on the hilltop," a man announced, running through the village. "He claims to be God and promises blessings to anyone who meets him. If you wish to see him, climb the hill."

The village buzzed with excitement. Everyone dropped their work and rushed to the hill, eager to meet the divine figure. People wanted to pour out their struggles, seek his blessings, and carry his gifts of grace home.

The hill was steep and challenging to climb, but the promise of meeting God inspired them to press on. Men, women, children, and elders—all climbed with unwavering determination.

Though they shared the same goal, the villagers split into groups, each carrying a flag of their faith. "Our God is the true one!" some proclaimed, while others argued, "No, ours is!" Tempers flared as they climbed, each group insisting on their version of God.

At the summit, they searched fervently. Sitting on a large rock was an old man. He looked worn and weathered, with disheveled hair, a long beard, and dusty, tattered clothes. In one hand, he held a staff for support; in the other, a begging bowl.

Disappointed, the villagers asked him, "Have you seen God? We've been searching everywhere."

He smiled. "I have seen him. Can't you?"

Confused, they replied, "We've scoured this hill and found no one. Where is he?"

He laughed heartily and said, "I am God."

The villagers were stunned. They thought he was either delusional or trying to deceive them. Anger flared, and they readied their flags as weapons to attack him. Sensing their rage, the man fled. They chased him, but he disappeared into thin air.

Standing helpless, they looked at one another in disbelief. Then a voice echoed from the cave:

"I am not mad—you are. I wanted to reveal the truth to you, but you chose to attack me. You think I've run away? How can I, when I am everything? I am all around you, within you. Listen carefully to my words, for they are the truth.

I am the reason for your existence. I planted the seed of your birth and gave you life. I nourish you, and one day, you will dissolve back into me.

I wander with a begging bowl, seeking your love. Yet you nurture hatred, divide yourselves, and give me countless names while fighting among yourselves. I could punish you, but instead, I hold my staff for support, not as a weapon. Yet you turn your sticks into weapons to harm the very one who sustains you."

"If you are truly God," they challenged, "why don't you face us boldly?"

"You stand on this hill, but you are smaller than it. The hill is smaller than the earth you live on. The earth is dwarfed by the sky, and the vast sky is nothing compared to the infinite cosmos I rule. I am the omnipresent force pervading everything. Your tiny eyes cannot see me."

"But we want to see you!" they pleaded. "Please reveal yourself."

"I am already within you. I am the love in your hearts, the compassion, peace, and patience you carry. I am the truth in your words. I am the divine light within your soul. Blinded by ignorance, you search for me in hills and caves, following deceitful promises, while ignoring the truth within you.

If you truly wish to see me, go home. Rest in your mother's lap. See me in her. When you honor your mother, you honor me. When you love her, you love me. The divine qualities of love, sacrifice, and compassion in your mother are my manifestations.

You run across the world, seeking me in vain, while I have been with you all along. Go home. Seek shelter in your mother's embrace. You will find me there."

With those words, the voice fell silent. A divine light illuminated the cave before vanishing.

The villagers stood still, their hearts stirred by newfound awareness. Among them, I, too, turned back. We descended the hill and returned home.

When I saw my mother, she appeared transformed—radiant, divine. Her glow filled my heart with realization: "Yes, those words were true. God resides in my mother."

To my astonishment, her light touched me too, and I began to glow. In her divine radiance, I found my own.

—·—·—●—·—·—

The Essence of Motherhood

During my college days, a group of friends and I planned an excursion. One of our beloved teachers, whom we all admired greatly, accompanied us. We were excited, dreaming of an enjoyable trip surrounded by nature's beauty.

Our teacher piqued our curiosity by saying, "What you're dreaming of is not the true destination. I'm taking you to a place beyond your imagination—a place so profound it will leave an indelible mark on your lives."

After a while, we reached our destination—a sprawling ashram nestled amidst nature's beauty. Surrounded by high walls, the ashram boasted blossoming gardens and a magnificent building that gleamed white under the sun. At the entrance, an elderly sage greeted us warmly.

Intrigued, we followed him inside. To our surprise, it was an orphanage.

The sage narrated the ashram's story—its origins, purpose, and the services it provided. The ashram was home to people from all walks of life: children born without parents, babies abandoned by mothers who suffered misfortunes, and elderly individuals cast out by their families.

The ashram was a haven where love flourished. There was no caste or religious discrimination, only mutual service and affection. It was a sanctuary for humanity, sustained entirely by the sage's personal resources.

We spent the day playing with the children, entertaining them, and offering what little service we could. We felt deeply fulfilled, as if our lives had found new meaning. Before leaving, we pledged to support the ashram's mission once we were established in life. We expressed heartfelt gratitude to our teacher for giving us the opportunity to serve.

Yet, on the way back, an unshakable sorrow lingered in my heart. I was haunted by the thought of their plight.

"They are not just orphans," I thought. "They are profoundly unfortunate souls. Without a mother's love, their lives must feel unbearably lonely. No matter how much they possess, a life without a mother is always incomplete."

When I returned home, I shared the details of our trip with my mother. I spoke at length about the orphans, expressing my pity for them. My mother, however, imparted a profound lesson that no book could ever teach.

"Motherhood," she said, "is not just a physical bond, my dear. The essence of motherhood lies in its qualities—love, compassion, care, sacrifice, patience, and tenderness. A woman who gives birth but lacks these virtues is not truly a mother; she is one in name only.

A flower that lacks fragrance, a cuckoo that cannot sing sweetly, a tree that bears no fruit, land that yields no crops, or clouds that bring no rain—these merely exist without purpose.

A mother is not just a person; she is a divine force present throughout the universe. In nature, we often hear tales of birds raising the chicks of other species, or animals nursing the young of another. In such cases, who is the true mother?

The Creator has instilled this nurturing essence throughout creation. Love, like air, water, and light, is freely available everywhere. True love knows no bounds, and God Himself is its ultimate embodiment. A mother is but a fragment of His infinite love.

Motherly love is limitless, my dear. It is not confined to one form or place—it is everywhere. Wherever you seek it, you will find it in abundance.

So, do not pity those you met at the ashram, thinking they lack a mother. Their teacher is both their father and mother. For those without guidance, God serves as their beacon. He is the shelter for the shelterless, the shade that cools the weary, and the steadfast friend who never abandons.

This, my dear, is the true meaning of motherhood. And this is the eternal truth."

My mother's words dispelled my sorrow and gave me a deeper understanding of life. From that day forward, I realized that motherhood is not confined to a single form but exists universally, as an eternal force of love and care.

'A-thiest'

"Can humans imprison the omnipresent God within four walls?

Did any deity ever declare a specific day—Sunday, Friday, or Saturday—as sacred?

While God proclaims His presence within us, why do you search the world for Him in ignorance?

Has God ever revealed a specific form to you?"

These were the questions I often posed, which led my friends to label me an atheist. They distanced themselves, leaving me alone and isolated.

Loneliness felt like a living hell. I pleaded with my friends to accept me back, to answer my questions, to restore our friendship. But they maintained their harsh stance, and I felt crushed under the weight of despair.

At a time when I longed for comfort, my mother—my eternal source of solace—was far away. I had moved away from her for higher studies. Silently, I prayed to her, asking for someone to fill the void left by her absence. Perhaps she heard my prayers because, soon after, I found a friend—a girl younger than me but with thoughts as profound as my mother's. Despite warnings from others to avoid me, she stayed by my side, her warm smile defying all criticism.

One day, I shared my grief with her, pouring my heart out. She listened and then asked, "The world is vast, isn't it? Why worry about a few people? Why cling to the hope that they must be your friends?"

When I couldn't answer, she continued, "If they were truly your friends, why did they leave you? Shouldn't they have sought to understand your questions and offered support? Were they ever truly your friends, or were you the only one invested in the friendship?"

I tried to explain, "I don't want enemies. Being branded an atheist and pushed away has been painful."

She fell silent for a moment, and then, with a calmness that radiated wisdom, she asked me nine questions:

Have you ever felt deeply moved by someone's life story?

Have you ever praised someone wholeheartedly, with genuine admiration?

Have you ever felt the urge to bow at someone's feet, overwhelmed by their greatness?

Have you ever given small gifts, like flowers or fruits, to someone just to honor them?

Have you ever felt like raising your hands in prayer or salutation at the sight of someone's radiance?

Have you ever longed to serve someone selflessly for the rest of your life?

Have you ever looked at someone and felt, "They are my true friend, the one who will share my joys and sorrows forever"?

Even in a crowd, has one person occupied your thoughts repeatedly?

Have you ever wished to dedicate your entire self to someone, becoming one with them?

I listened to her questions, closed my eyes, and reflected deeply. As if by instinct, the word "Mother" escaped my lips. When I opened my eyes, my friend was smiling at me.

"You are no atheist," she said gently. "In fact, you are the truest believer. Now, go back to your friends. Share with them your thoughts about your mother. Explain to them the essence of devotion and its deeper meaning. Help them understand that the real God resides within us, and in your case, within your love for your mother. Show them the truth. Go now."

Her words were like divine guidance, and I felt like a mere instrument in her hands. I did as she instructed.

When I approached my friends and shared my thoughts, they initially turned away. For a few moments, there was silence. Feeling disheartened, I began to leave.

Then, a booming voice called out, "Friend, wait!" Turning around, I saw my friends looking at me with new eyes.

"You are not unworthy of our friendship… you are not an atheist. In truth, you are a greater believer than any of us. If you think we are worthy of being your friends, we humbly ask you to accept us."

Their words sent a wave of joy through me. I ran to them, embraced them, and felt a profound sense of belonging. Surrounded by my friends, I was no longer alone. In that moment, we found unity, harmony, and shared bliss.

The Beauty of Blindness

One day, I was walking along a busy road, eager to cross over to the other side. The road was chaotic with vehicles rushing by, creating a cacophony of sounds. Beside me, a woman was also trying to navigate her way across. She was blind, unable to see the world but relying on her other senses to perceive it.

Moved by her struggle, I approached her and held her hand to guide her safely to the other side. With a sense of satisfaction, I sighed in relief after helping her. Just as I was about to leave, she stopped me with a question.

"Why did you hold my hand and guide me? Was it out of love or pity?" she asked.

Surprised, I replied, "Why would I love someone whose face I don't even recognize? And you're just a beggar. Don't overthink it—it was out of pity for you being blind."

"Pity? Why would you pity me?"

"Because I can see the beautiful world around me, and you cannot," I said matter-of-factly.

"Is that so? But can you see the beautiful world that I perceive? In my eyes, you are just as blind as I am," she retorted.

Her words struck me like lightning, leaving me speechless. I had no answer, so I walked away in silence. Her question, however, lingered in my mind for days, haunting me with its profundity.

Unable to shake it off, I returned to the same road in search of her. When I finally found her, I approached and gently held her hand.

To my astonishment, she said, "Ah, you've come back, my friend."

"How did you know it was me?" I asked, amazed.

"My friend, I may be blind, but four of my senses still work perfectly. In many ways, I am more complete than you," she replied with a soft laugh.

In that moment, she seemed to me like a sage, someone far wiser than I could ever hope to be. Humbled, I asked, "Will you allow me to be your friend?"

"Friendship isn't something we allow or disallow," she said. "Everyone on this earth is connected, whether they realize it or not. Come, walk with me," she said, extending her hand.

As I walked with her, I realized something profound—though she was blind, she was leading me. My sense of superiority shattered, I understood that I had more to learn from her than she did from me.

Over time, we became close friends. Many ridiculed me for befriending a beggar, but I ignored their mockery. "Don't judge a person by their appearance; look into their soul," I'd say, standing by my friendship with her. Despite her young age, she taught me life lessons I'd never imagined.

"How do you know so much about life?" I asked her one day.

"I've learned it all from nature," she said.

Though I was astonished, her explanation left me even more in awe:

"I can tell if my path is right or wrong just by the feel of the ground beneath my feet. The wind tells me about the changes in the environment. By the air I breathe, I sense the nature of people around me. By their words, I understand their thoughts. I know light through warmth and darkness through silence.

You all yearn for friendship with humans, but I seek companionship with all creatures. For me, the earth is my bed, rocks are my pillows, trees provide shade, rain quenches my thirst, and the air is my lifebreath. Even in darkness, I feel the comfort of light, and my silent friends—animals—keep me company."

Her words astounded me. "What is the purpose of your life?" I asked.

"God gave me breath, so I must live. He blessed me with a beautiful child, and I must nurture him until he grows wings to fly. That's my purpose—to live."

"You have a child? How?" I asked, shocked.

"In this world, there are not just animals and birds but also beasts in human form. Why is it surprising that I gave birth?" she said with a wry smile.

"Where is your child now?" I asked.

"He's swinging in a cradle hung on a tree at the edge of the village," she replied.

"Who watches over him?"

"I told you—nature. Nature protects him. The animals around him form a shield until I return. If anyone dares to harm him, they would tear that person apart."

"What's your name?" I asked.

"I don't know. But my child calls me 'Mother.' That must be my name. It's only after becoming a mother that I truly understood the world. I realized who my protector is, and I discovered the love within me—all because I became a mother."

That day, she released my hand and walked away, leaving me with profound truths about life. She didn't just teach me about motherhood; she revealed the essence of existence itself. Through her, I finally understood what it meant to be truly alive.

Nature's Rejoinder

Do happiness and sorrow truly exist, or are they mere constructs of our imagination? Are they rooted in karma, driven by desires, or are they simply emotions shaped by perception? Is the life we experience a manifestation of reality, or just fleeting sensations?

Why does one person feel restless even when flying in an airplane, while another person finds boundless joy walking barefoot on the ground? Are problems real, or are they self-created?

These questions have followed me throughout my journey of life. I've encountered countless people, experiences, and events, feeling overwhelmed by their vastness, believing they had no end.

There was a phase in my life when I found myself submerged in extreme stress—an abyss devoid of light. Financial struggles, mental turmoil, helplessness, and loneliness surrounded me like an impenetrable fog of darkness.

Failures, ridicule, and humiliation—uninvited companions— took permanent residence in my life. I was trapped, directionless, amidst the crossroads of uncertainty.

People would listen but never offer solutions. Words of comfort came aplenty, but no action. In those moments, I thought of my mother, the only person capable of unraveling even the tightest knots with a single smile, exuding calmness without a shred of arrogance.

But during this tumultuous period, I was physically distant from her. The passing moments felt like endless ages, filling me with anguish. I longed for her presence, but it was impossible. I had no choice but to face my questions alone, carrying the heavy burden of existence.

One of her teachings echoed in my mind:

"If ever a time comes when I cannot reach you or you cannot reach me, remember this truth—when questions arise within you, do not expect answers from others."

One evening, overwhelmed with the weight of my thoughts, I set out aimlessly, walking with no destination in mind. I kept walking until I arrived at a place so beautiful it felt like stepping into another realm.

The place seemed magical, as though it welcomed me with open arms, whispering, *"You are not alone; you are one of us."*

The air filled me with hope and breathed new life into me. The unyielding light, devoid of shadows, revealed the beauty of tomorrow. A flowing stream murmured that even problems are like its waters—always moving, never stagnant. The songs of birds entered my ears like a soothing balm, stealing away my sorrows. Graceful deer grazing nearby melted my despair, filling my eyes with calm. Footprints of past travelers hinted at perseverance, urging me to move forward. A towering tree, firm and proud, seemed to mock me: *"I have withstood storms and remained upright. Are you so fragile that you collapse repeatedly?"*

Even tiny fish swimming tirelessly in puddles, darting back and forth, seemed to offer wisdom.

With every passing moment, my fears began to fade. Strength and confidence, long suppressed, began to resurface. Each sight carried beauty, and each beauty carried a lesson. A memory from my mother emerged clearly in my mind, filling me with newfound courage:

"When I am not by your side, nature itself becomes your mother. When your father cannot guide you, nature becomes your father. Beyond books, nature becomes the teacher who reveals truths. Always love and cherish nature, for it alone will comfort you and embrace you like the divine."

Filled with this profound conviction, I returned from that place. As I walked back, my mother's favorite song echoed in my mind, guiding me forward:

"Life …..

Is a song that blooms like flowers

Marching forward with fiery steps

Drenching in the showers of hopes

Making friendship with cool brazes

Running through the fields of crops

Scattering, falling, rising dreams

Renews itself as a spring blossoms

A beautiful journey that ever flees."

In that moment, I realized that life itself is both the question and the answer. Nature, in its infinite wisdom, holds the key to healing and guidance for those who seek it.

Glad Tidings

One evening, I noticed my father pacing restlessly around the house. It was well past midnight, yet he couldn't sleep. His unease was evident, and I couldn't help but wonder—was he unwell, or was he troubled by some pressing issue? I decided to approach him.

"Father, are you unable to sleep? Are you feeling alright? Why are you so worried? You're making me anxious. Please tell me," I said.

My father looked at me and then at his bed, his expression switching between sorrow and helplessness. "Yes," he nodded softly, his demeanor akin to that of a lost child.

"It's been a week since your mother went to visit her hometown. I've never been without her for this long. During the day, I can distract myself with work, but the nights feel unbearably heavy," he admitted, his eyes welling with tears.

My father—an otherwise towering figure of strength— seemed so vulnerable in that moment. I was just a ten-year-old boy, unprepared to console my father. The scene is etched in my memory as one of profound emotional connection.

"Father, I miss our mother too. But why are you more troubled than I am? Shouldn't children miss their mother more than fathers?" I asked innocently.

My father gave a faint smile and led me to his room. He sat me beside him on the bed and began to explain.

"Son, you're still a child, so it's natural for you to think that way. But for a man, his wife becomes his entire world the moment they marry. She is his mother, friend, confidant, and partner in everything. She's not just his companion; she's his entire existence."

"She is the light of the house, illuminating it with her presence. She observes her husband's needs, transforming the home into a sanctuary. She eases his burdens with her gentle words, much like a soothing balm for his troubles. Like a mother, she nourishes him with care and helps him find rest. She rests her head on his chest, leading him into dreams filled with peace. Even when he's irritable or upset, she responds with patience and kindness. That's the divinity of a wife."

"And now, all of this is missing from my life. I find myself waiting, longing for her return," he confessed, his voice tinged with melancholy.

"Doesn't Mother miss you too, Father?" I asked.

"My heart is with her, and her heart is with me. Though we are physically apart, we communicate in silence. Still, this physical separation weighs heavily," he replied.

"Then why did you let her go to her hometown, Father? Couldn't you have asked her to stay?" I questioned further.

"When we married, I made a vow. I promised to honor her wishes and never deny her happiness. I vowed to be her support, her protector, and her companion, forever faithful. These vows were made not just in her presence but before everyone, and I've remained true to them," he said with pride.

"But can't we visit her now? I'll come with you," I suggested enthusiastically.

"That's exactly what I was thinking. Let's leave tomorrow morning," he agreed, his face lighting up.

That night, I slept beside my father, filling the space left by my mother. We found solace in each other's presence and drifted into a peaceful sleep.

The next morning, we woke up early, got ready, and packed our bags. Just as we were locking the house, the postman arrived with a postcard. Handing it to me, he left quickly. I glanced at the card—it was from my mother.

"Father! Mother is coming back today!" I shouted excitedly, my voice brimming with joy.

Hearing this, my father dropped the luggage from both hands, fell to his knees, and began to cry like a child. I stood there, astonished, watching him shed tears of happiness.

To know that the woman he loved with all his heart was returning brought him immense joy—so much so that it overwhelmed him. As a child, I couldn't fully comprehend the depth of his emotions.

Now, as a grown man, I understand. Every time I find myself apart from my wife—the woman who loves and cares for me like a mother—I recall that moment with my father.

The joy of having the woman you love by your side is an experience that my father, I, and every man cherishes deeply, forever etched in our hearts.

Lovely Fabrication

My mother possessed a rare, unparalleled ability—a gift to perceive and uncover hidden potential in people with just her gaze. Her heart brimmed with love, reaching out to embrace others and gently encouraging them with a compassionate touch. That golden heart was her true treasure.

One day, an unusual incident unfolded. A stranger arrived at our home, seemingly out of nowhere. He called my mother by name, knelt before her, and began narrating his story. He claimed to have no home, no family, and spoke of being abandoned by his loved ones. He hadn't eaten in days and was drowning in endless suffering. His tale painted a picture of despair.

My mother, like melting wax, was moved. Without hesitation, she removed one of her gold bangles and handed it to him. I was taken aback. Had she been deceived by his words? I thought her boundless kindness had gone too far, yet I couldn't find the courage to intervene.

The stranger received the bangle with folded hands, offered countless thanks, and left. My mother watched him leave, her gaze filled with love and compassion. Mustering all my courage, I finally spoke up.

"Mother, he deceived you! That was a made-up story! How could someone as wise as you fall for his lies?"

"Yes, son, I knew it was all fabricated," she replied calmly. "But go, find him and bring him back to me."

Confused but obedient, I ran to search for the man. After much effort, I found him in a bar, having sold the bangle and spending the money on food and drink. Furious, I grabbed him by his shirt and dragged him back home, throwing him at my mother's feet.

He looked up at her with guilt-ridden eyes. My mother, however, lifted him gently and spoke with her usual warmth.

I stood there, bewildered. Was she about to be fooled again?

Then she began to speak, her words full of wisdom:

"Son, you told me lies. You think you deceived me, but in truth, you are deceiving yourself. You possess a remarkable talent. The story you spun was woven with such skill and emotion that it captured my attention entirely. You have the gift of storytelling, a light in your eyes, and wisdom painted by life's experiences.

"Right now, you use this gift to manipulate others for temporary gain. But the guilt of wrongdoing will always shadow you. Harness this talent for good. Share your stories with the world, not to deceive, but to inspire. Stand tall, live with pride, and shine like the sun that spreads light to all. Live not just for yourself but for others, and give meaning to your life. Go, may you find your path."

The man, who had come fearing punishment, received the gift of guidance instead. He left, transformed by her words.

A year passed, and one day, an unfamiliar but dignified man appeared at our doorstep. I asked him who he was.

"I've come to meet my guru. Please allow me to see her," he replied.

"Who is your guru?" I asked.

"Your mother," he said. "The one who transformed my life."

Startled, I led him inside. He bowed at my mother's feet, tears streaming down his face. After a moment, he began speaking.

"Mother, your words that day changed my life forever. You took in a deceiver like me and awakened me to my potential. Today, I stand before you as a successful writer, earning respect and accolades across the nation. I've published countless stories under the pen name *Amma* (Mother). Every recognition I've received is because of you. I owe my new life to your love and guidance. Please accept this gold bangle as a token of my gratitude."

He presented a new gold bangle to her, but my mother gently refused.

"If I expected something in return, how could it be called a mother's love?" she said.

The man's eyes brimmed with tears, while my mother's face radiated joy.

As I stood there witnessing the profound moment, I felt like a child again, marveling at the boundless love and wisdom of my mother, the true embodiment of a golden heart.

The Gift of the Heart

As a child, I celebrated many birthdays, each marked by my mother's thoughtful gifts, which never failed to fill me with joy. To this day, I have carefully preserved many of those treasures.

One day, as I sat admiring them, reliving the memories attached, a particular birthday came to mind, flooding me with emotions. It was my twelfth birthday. That year, my mother gave me a special gift, one I proudly showed off to my friends.

But amidst the admiration, one friend asked, "You always receive gifts. Have you ever thought of giving your mother a birthday gift to make her happy?"

The question planted a seed in my mind. The thought lingered, and soon, the day arrived—it was my mother's birthday. Determined to surprise her with a divine gift, I pondered endlessly about what would make her happiest.

That night, I lay under the open sky, trying to decide. Images of possible gifts swirled in my mind, each appearing and fading like a fleeting dream.

A bouquet of flowers stood before me, radiant in its beauty. "But you'll wilt by evening," I thought, dismissing it.

Next came a glittering gold ornament, dazzling in its brilliance. "You have no life; you cannot touch my mother's heart," I said, rejecting it.

A beautiful parrot landed on my shoulder, chirping as if to ask, "Shall I be the gift?" "My mother wouldn't like to see a free creature caged. Fly away to your freedom," I replied.

The moonlight bathed me in its gentle glow. "Can I be the gift?" it seemed to ask. "Your brilliance pales in comparison to my mother's smile," I said.

A magnificent peacock spread its feathers before me. "I'll dance to delight her," it offered. "But my mother's graceful steps outshine even the grandest of peacock dances," I replied.

Thus, the entire night passed as I debated and dismissed every possibility. By morning, despair set in. None of the gifts felt worthy of my mother. For someone who had given me countless gifts and joy, I couldn't find one suitable offering.

As the first light of dawn crept in, my mother stirred. Overwhelmed by helplessness, I ran to her and wrapped my arms around her. Tears streamed down my face, soaking her heart as I cried my heart out.

My mother held me close, wiping away my tears with a gentle smile. Her voice, filled with love, reached my ears like divine music—words that only a mother could utter:

"My dear child, why do you say you couldn't give me a gift when you've already given me the most precious one? Is there a more divine gift in this world than your loving embrace?

Your tiny arms around my neck are like garlands of mandara flowers adorning me. The determined steps you took to reach me felt like a peacock's graceful dance. Your soft breaths are like a melodious flute, and the rhythm of your heartbeat against mine is a sweet hymn of blessings.

The tears that fell from your eyes are no less than sacred nectar showering upon me. No worldly gift could ever match the love and devotion you've shown me. You've made me the richest mother on earth, my child!"

Her words, unique to mothers and filled with unparalleled affection, echoed in my heart. Even now, they resonate in my soul, transforming my life into a perpetual spring of love and gratitude.

The Beautiful Thief

During my childhood, a peculiar series of thefts occurred in our home. It wasn't just a one-time incident but a continuous enigma that baffled us all. Who were the thieves? How were they entering our house? When were they stealing? None of these questions had answers, leaving the mystery unsolved.

My father, frustrated, replaced four different domestic helpers, hoping to stop the thefts. Yet, the strange occurrences continued. Money mysteriously disappeared from his wallet, and after some time, he seemed to stop caring altogether.

One day, I overheard my parents discussing the matter.

"I have no idea how the money keeps vanishing," my father said, perplexed. "But it seems futile to worry about it now. No matter how much I leave in my wallet, only some of it gets stolen. It's all so confusing."

My mother remained silent for a moment before speaking softly, "God is kind. If He takes something, He gives something more in return. Don't worry."

My father chuckled, while I stood nearby, stunned.

Could it be that they were suspecting me? Were they laughing because they thought I was the thief? I was overwhelmed by a sense of shame and injustice. Though I had no involvement, I felt accused. Determined to clear my name, I resolved to catch the culprit.

Night after night, I stayed awake, hoping to catch the thief red-handed. Yet, the mystery only deepened. Everyone in the house, including the domestic help, seemed oblivious. Meanwhile, the thefts persisted.

What puzzled me even more was my father's indifferent attitude. Why wasn't he more concerned? Why did he simply brush it off?

Finally, after four days of relentless effort, I discovered the thief. But what I saw left me utterly speechless.

The thief was none other than my mother!

I ran to my father to tell him what I had seen. "It's impossible!" he exclaimed. "Your mother is no thief. Don't accuse her without proof. Observe carefully before jumping to conclusions."

Though disheartened by his dismissal, I resolved to gather undeniable evidence.

A few days later, I witnessed my mother in the act. She carefully packed clothes, food, and other supplies into a bag and discreetly but confidently took money from my father's wallet. Then, she slipped out of the house.

Determined to uncover the truth, I followed her. Where was she going with those stolen goods?

She walked a long way until she reached a small settlement. It was a shelter for orphans.

As soon as she arrived, the children swarmed around her, calling out, "Mother! Mother!" She lovingly distributed everything she had brought, ensuring everyone received their share. She embraced them with such affection, crossing all divides of caste and status, that my heart trembled with emotion.

I stood there, watching in awe as my mother listened to their stories, comforted them, and gave them hope. To those children, she was not just a visitor—she was their mother.

A wave of guilt washed over me. How ignorant and foolish I had been to suspect my mother. She wasn't just my mother—she was a mother to all!

Silently, I left the place and went straight to my father. I narrated everything I had witnessed, expecting him to be as surprised as I had been. But to my astonishment, he simply smiled.

"I already knew," he said calmly.

"Then why did you say there were thefts in the house?"

"Because every time I mentioned it, she would look away shyly, trying to hide her smile. It's a sight I cherish."

"But isn't theft wrong?" I asked, still puzzled.

"She is the mistress of this house," he replied. "Taking something from her own home is not theft—it's her freedom. Everything in this house, including you and me, is her wealth."

"Still, couldn't she have told us?"

"Giving doesn't require an announcement, my son. Only taking does."

My father's words opened my eyes to a new understanding. I realized the profound depth of my mother's character. She wasn't just a giver—she was love personified.

From that day forward, I saw her in a new light, as a beacon of selfless love. She was not just my mother—she was the heart of our home and the soul of those children's lives.

—·—·—●—·—·—

Eternal Youth

One day, my mother, father, and I were sitting together, sipping coffee and chatting lightheartedly. The air was filled with laughter and joy.

While my mother was speaking, I noticed my father looking at her intently. After a while, she turned to him and asked, "What's on your mind?"

"I see two strands of white hair gleaming among your black locks. You're getting older," he said with a smile.

"I always walk behind you. If I have two, you must have four," she replied with a chuckle.

They both burst into laughter, their faces glowing like blooming flowers. It was a heartwarming sight, filling me with the sensation of being in a beautiful garden.

Later, I went to my room, but the scene lingered in my mind, playing over and over like a delightful memory. However, as time passed, other thoughts began to sprout, creeping in like dark clouds and casting shadows over my heart.

"Is mother really growing older? Does that mean she's moving from youth to old age? Will her radiant beauty, like a lotus in a serene pond, begin to fade? Will the petals of her bloom fall one by one? Like everyone else, will she also leave me and this world behind, embarking on a journey to the beyond?

Will I be left alone, without her comforting presence? Will I never again hear her sweet laughter or her divine words? Will the ocean of her compassion dry up? Will the stream of her love cease to flow? Will the hand that guides me leave mine forever?

The thought of her departing, of losing my guiding star, was unbearable. Is there no way to pause time? No way to keep her eternally youthful?"

These thoughts tormented me, making it hard to breathe. My heart felt heavy, and tears streamed down my face like an unstoppable rain.

Slowly, I walked toward my mother. She was seated in a meditative pose, immersed in a state of tranquility. She looked like a philosopher, a deep ocean, and a steadfast mountain, all at once.

I gently rested my head on her lap. She opened her eyes, placed her hands on my shoulders, and lifted me up. Observing the worry etched on my face, she wiped my tear-streaked cheeks. Her eyes, filled with compassion, silently questioned me.

Unable to contain my anguish, I poured out my fears and began sobbing like a child.

"Mother! Are you going to grow old? Will you leave me behind? Will you abandon me to face life alone? Will there come a time when my life will be engulfed in darkness because you're no longer with me?"

Hearing my despair, my mother laughed heartily. "No, my child. A mother never grows old. She is forever youthful. I will never leave you. I am eternal," she said reassuringly.

"Mother! The thought of you aging, losing strength, and one day leaving this world fills me with boundless sorrow. If there is a way to keep you forever youthful, please tell me. I will do whatever it takes to preserve you."

Listening to my plea, my mother began to speak. Her words flowed like sacred chants, like the melody of a thousand veenas played in harmony. Each word dispelled my sorrow and revealed profound truths about life and the mysteries of creation.

"My dear child, a mother is a divine force. Your mother is one, but 'Mother' is another. Motherhood is eternal and universal. It is the source of all creation. From the smallest ant to the infinite cosmos, every being has a mother. Without a mother, there is no birth. Motherhood is life itself. Even the divine owes its birth to Mother. A mother is like a fountain of nectar, a symbol of immortality.

I, too, have a mother. I am your mother, and your children will have their mother. Their children will have theirs, and so on. This chain of motherhood is an unbroken gift of existence.

We all come to this earth for a brief sojourn, to rest and partake in life's beauty, before merging back into creation. This truth is what the divine constantly teaches us.

Where would I go, my dear? Only my body will leave. I, as a mother, will be reborn as your child. I will fill your life with light, love you, walk beside you, and repay the care you've given me. Let go of your worries. Every moment is a blessing. Experience it fully and live joyfully, my child."

Her words, like a warm embrace, lifted the veil of despair from my heart. That day, I realized that a mother's love transcends time, and her essence is eternal.

Justice of Maternal Love

After a long time, I decided to visit my childhood friend. While many of us tied our lives to jobs and businesses, exhausted from the hustle, he stayed true to his roots. He never left his village or farming and dedicated his life to the soil, living peacefully and contentedly.

When I arrived, my friend was in his courtyard, feeding the chickens. He greeted me warmly, embraced me, and we sat together, chatting about old times.

As we talked, I noticed the chickens moving around in an orderly manner, pecking at the grains he scattered. Suddenly, a hen appeared, strutting gracefully, leading a small flock of chicks. The other chickens made way for her, respecting her presence. The mother hen first let her chicks eat, standing watchfully, and then ate herself before moving on with her little ones trailing behind like an obedient army.

As they played together, the hen climbed onto a small rock, keeping a watchful eye over her brood. It was a delightful sight, filling me with joy.

Out of nowhere, a kite swooped down from the sky, trying to snatch one of the chicks. In an instant, the mother hen rose to the challenge, chasing the kite into the sky. She flew higher than I ever thought a hen could, forcing the kite to retreat to the heavens. The hen then descended back to her perch, scanning the sky with a fierce gaze, her stance reminiscent of a cobra ready to strike.

I was stunned. "I've never seen a hen fly so high!" I exclaimed in amazement.

"It's a mother hen," my friend replied calmly. "When her chicks are threatened, she gathers strength she didn't know she had. Protecting her offspring is what every mother does naturally. My father used to call this the 'Justice of the Hen and Chick.'"

"Justice? Do even animals and birds have justice systems?" I asked, intrigued.

"They do," he nodded. "And not just justice, but lessons of love and sacrifice that bind mothers and offspring together. Want to hear more?"

Eager to learn, I urged him to continue.

"Consider the turtle. It lays its eggs in the sand and returns to the water, leaving its offspring behind. Yet, through mere thought, it nurtures the eggs, guiding them to hatch. When the hatchlings emerge, they instinctively head toward the water, where they eventually meet their mother. This is known as *Kurma Kishora Nyaya* (The Justice of the Turtle and Hatchling). Though physically apart, the connection of thought unites them.

Monkeys, on the other hand, cling tightly to their mothers as she leaps from branch to branch. The mother doesn't hold onto them; it's the young ones who grip her firmly. This is called *Markata Kishora Nyaya* (The Justice of the Monkey and Young). It teaches that children must depend on their mothers for survival.

Cats carry their kittens in their mouths, relocating them to safer places. The mother ensures their protection at all times. This is called *Marjala Kishora Nyaya* (The Justice of the Cat and Kitten). It illustrates the mother's relentless effort to safeguard her young.

In the case of cows, they are always seen standing close to their calves, nurturing them with constant proximity and care. This is called *Go Kishora Nyaya* (The Justice of the Cow and Calf). The mother ensures her offspring's safety and guidance by staying close.

These laws of nature, passed down by our ancestors, describe the love and duty of mothers toward their children. Each mother, whether bird or beast, follows these principles for a while, nurturing her young until they can fend for themselves. Then, she lets them go to live independently. Have you noticed how birds do the same? This is the eternal cycle of life and love between mothers and children," my friend concluded.

For a while, silence settled between us. My thoughts wandered to the beauty and depth of what I had just heard.

"Wow! How incredible!" I finally exclaimed. "These principles of justice and care are all present in my own mother! Aren't they in yours too? In fact, they're in every mother. The love of a mother is the amalgamation of all these forms of care. While animals' love is finite, a mother's love is infinite. She is the divine force that showers us with unconditional love throughout our lives. All these forms of justice you spoke of merge into one: *Motherhood*. Thank you, my friend, for indirectly helping me realize the divinity of a mother."

With that, I bid him farewell, my heart brimming with newfound reverence for mothers everywhere.

Path of Words

It had just stopped raining. The roads were still wet, and my mother and I were walking hand in hand along the side of the road. I was carefully guiding her to ensure she didn't slip, and she was doing the same for me.

Suddenly, a vehicle zoomed past us, splashing muddy water all over us. Our clothes were drenched. Anger bubbled up inside me. I shouted at the driver, cursing him loudly.

My mother held my hand firmly, looked at me with a gentle smile, and asked, "Can't you control yourself?"

"But, Mom! It was his fault. Why should I stay quiet?" I argued.

"It could be a man, or a woman, or someone else in that vehicle. Do you know who it was? Do you know why they were in such a hurry? Maybe it was an emergency, or perhaps they were anxious. If it was carelessness, it reflects their inner turmoil or immaturity. Why are you getting so agitated?" she asked calmly.

"But, Mom! Because of him, we're drenched. Our clothes are ruined!"

"And will your anger dry your clothes, my dear? Anger doesn't help. Instead, think about your own actions. Should you have been walking so close to the road after rain? If your urgency is justified, maybe theirs is too. Changing clothes will solve the problem, but what will your anger achieve other than creating harmful vibrations within you? Let's move on, son; your destination lies ahead."

With those words, she resumed walking. I followed her, deep in thought. Then she shared an invaluable lesson with me:

"Anger shouldn't arise unnecessarily. If it does, let it be for a purpose. The only valid anger is the kind that brings about good for others."

She continued, "Rama's anger brought justice to the world. Krishna's anger upheld dharma. But Christ did not become angry; if he had, the cross would have been shattered. Buddha could have conquered kingdoms with his wisdom, yet he chose peace and compassion instead. Righteousness, kindness, and patience—these should be our ornaments at all times."

As life moved forward, her words gradually became clear to me. Since that incident, I've rarely been consumed by anger.

Another unforgettable experience with my mother was the turning point in my life, setting me on a path of purpose.

One day, I was sitting alone, feeling dejected. Anxiety had replaced all my enthusiasm. My mother noticed my state and asked, "Why do you look so downhearted?"

"Mom, the way the world is today fills me with fear. The wars, the violence, the destruction—they make me feel hopeless. I worry about the survival of humanity itself. Why are these wars, both external and internal, happening? Who benefits from all this devastation? How can the world be changed? How can these atrocities be stopped? Thinking about it all makes me feel lost and overwhelmed," I confessed.

Hearing my words, she smiled gently.

"Your thoughts are racing beyond your reach, son. That's why you feel so troubled. Standing on the ground, you're trying to measure the height of a mountain. Can you see the far shore of an ocean while sitting on this one? Think within your limits, and you'll find solutions. Or, rise to a global level, and you may transform the world. For now, focus on your own responsibilities. Worrying about others' duties will only burden you and instill fear. Work for your own welfare and for those around you. That will bring you peace and satisfaction.

"Wars and calamities have always happened and will continue to happen. Stopping them is beyond the power of any single individual. Start by uplifting yourself. The day every person does this, the world will naturally find its balance. Plan your actions so they benefit everyone. That will bring you true joy. Overthinking beyond your capacity can be dangerous, my dear."

Her words became the guiding light of my life. I began planning my actions in ways that would benefit others. The anxiety within me dissolved, replaced by hope for a better world. With dreams of a brighter future, I have been moving forward, one meaningful step at a time.

—·—·—●—·—·—

A Sacral Treasure

«Mom, I have such a wonderful mother. A beautiful mother. A mother who is like a goddess. A mother so great that I feel there's nothing I need in life but her. But, Mom, do you have a mother too?"

This was the innocent question I asked my mom as a child. Hearing my question, my mom laughed wholeheartedly. Her eyes brimmed with tears of joy, and her heart swelled with emotion. She pulled me close, caressed my head, and replied:

"I do, dear. Without a mother, there would be no birth in this universe."

"Where is your mother now? I've never seen her."

"Our mother has transformed into a child once again, playing blissfully in the divine realms of God."

"Then who is your mother's mother? And her mother? Are they all playing as children there?"

"Yes, dear, that's how it is. 'Mother' is not just a person—it's a divine light, a heavenly gift. It passes from one woman to another, generation after generation, from time immemorial.

Motherhood is not limited to humans alone. This radiant light extends even to insects, animals, and birds. Without mothers, there would be no creation, no life."

Her words planted a profound truth in my young heart: Motherhood is a universal, divine force. Over time, this understanding deepened, becoming a foundation for my immense respect and reverence for all mothers, and for women everywhere.

A Philosophical Debate

A peculiar debate often played in my mind as I grew older: Who is greater—God or Mother?

God gives us life, but Mother protects it. God creates love, but Mother spreads it and nourishes it. God gives us grain, but Mother prepares it into food. God creates paths, but Mother leads us along them. God pours rain, but Mother quenches our thirst. God's presence is elusive—reachable only through penance—but Mother is ever-present, visible, and tangible. Compared to a God who responds when called, a Mother who loves without being summoned feels infinitely greater.

Yet, sometimes I would think, "Isn't God, who gave us such a divine Mother, even greater?" This debate would continue in my mind, but one undeniable truth stood firm:

"A Mother, who can stand as an equal to God and even surpass Him, is the most extraordinary being."

Mother as the Quintessence of the Elements

The universe is composed of five fundamental elements: air, water, fire, space, and earth. These elements sustain all life. But the ability to absorb these elements and turn them into life-giving sustenance belongs only to a Mother.

Air: As a baby forms in her womb, a mother becomes the air that breathes life into it, making its heart beat.

Water: Her blood transforms into milk to nourish the baby.

Fire: Her warmth envelops the child, offering comfort and security.

Space: Like the vast sky, her love knows no boundaries.

Earth: She becomes the foundation of the child's life, nurturing with the patience and endurance of the Earth itself.

Loving and respecting a Mother is equivalent to honoring these five elements.

A Universal Force

Motherhood transcends individual existence. Some believe in God; others deny Him. But both groups agree on one truth: Everyone has a Mother. This truth is undeniable.

Motherhood is a divine light, as eternal as the sun and moon. Generations may pass, eras may change, but this light continues to shine.

As long as there is womanhood, the essence of Motherhood will illuminate the Earth. Even God relies on this force—be it Krishna with Yashoda and Devaki, Rama with Kausalya, Buddha with Maya, or Christ with Mary. Every divine being owes their roots to a Mother.

What they brought to the world was the essence of Mother's love. A Mother's presence, in visible form or as the divine energy within all beings, is an eternal truth that sustains the world.

Home Vs Temple

After my father passed away, my mother was left alone. I wanted to bring her with me, away from the house my father had built. But she refused to leave the home that carried his memories. I thought it might help if I turned her thoughts toward spirituality.

"Mom, I want to spend a month with you. Let's travel across the country together," I pleaded. Finally, she agreed.

On a bright morning, we set out on our journey. We visited the temple of Lord Rama, where I explained the essence of his boundless love. She listened like a child, enraptured by my words. Next, we explored the beautiful gardens where Lord Krishna had played, and I narrated stories of his childhood. She was captivated.

We visited churches and relived the compassionate stories of Christ. We explored mosques, where I helped her experience the serene atmosphere of prayer. In Buddhist monasteries, I explained the peace-filled teachings of Buddha. We even visited local shrines and delved into the meanings of diverse beliefs. I left no spiritual corner untouched.

By the end of the month, my mother seemed more at peace. I was content with my efforts. When we returned home, I asked, "Mom, don't you feel lighter now? Isn't your heart more at ease?"

"Yes, my child," she replied. "These thirty days have been so peaceful. My heart felt as though it was floating, unburdened. I'm truly happy."

Encouraged, I said, "After some time, I'll come back, and we'll visit even more new places. You should stay calm and content. That's all I wish for, Mom. Shall I leave now? I have many pending tasks to finish."

"Yes, go ahead, my dear," she said. "But since we've visited so many sacred places, your father might return to us now, won't he?"

Her question struck me deeply.

"Mom, can those who've departed ever come back? Just now, you said you feel at peace. Why this strange question now?"

"Then tell me, what purpose did all our journeys serve? Why spend so much time, energy, and money?"

"It was only to bring you peace and ease the weight in your heart, Mom. Didn't you know that? I took you on this journey believing that spiritual strength would heal your soul."

"My home—the breeze within it, the light it offers—gives me more peace than any sacred place we visited. This house, my dear, is the temple where my god, your father, lived. The memories of my time with him are my solace, my lullaby. Every wall of this house whispers his words to me, sweet and comforting. No spiritual center I've seen can compare to this home. No deity elsewhere could reveal themselves more than he does here."

Her words carried profound meaning, even though they took me by surprise.

"Then why did you say you felt at peace, Mom? Was that just to make me happy?"

"No, dear, I didn't lie. These thirty days truly brought me joy and tranquility. But it wasn't because of the holy places. It was because you were by my side, traveling with me. That's what brought me happiness."

Her words touched my heart deeply. My mother held countless truths, each profound. She was a philosopher, a wise soul, and far beyond my understanding. My attempts to bring her solace only revealed how naive and childlike I was. I found myself speechless. Bowing to her feet, I prepared to leave.

My mother held my hands tenderly, her eyes glistening with unshed tears.

"Don't be disheartened, my child. Your efforts were not in vain, nor was our journey wasted. God is compassionate. He will surely grant our prayer. Your father will return to us soon, bringing joy and light to our home once again."

"How is that possible, Mom?"

"It is possible, my dear. Your father will return—as your child. At every sacred place we visited, I prayed for this. It will surely happen. God is merciful. Go now."

In that moment, my mother seemed like a deity herself. Praying that her wish would come true, I bowed to her and departed with a heart full of joy and hope.

A Saintly Wish

It had been a while since I last visited my mother. One day, I received a letter from her. It said, "It's been so long since I've seen you. Please come and visit, my child. I have something important to discuss." The letter left me puzzled. What could be so significant that she couldn't write it down? After much thought, I decided to go see her in person.

When I arrived, my mother's face lit up with joy. She welcomed me warmly, and we spent some time together. I didn't want to rush her, so I waited until the next day to ask, "Mom, why did you call me? What is the matter?"

She smiled gently. "I called you because I wanted to talk to you," she replied.

Knowing my mother well, I realized she wouldn't disrupt my busy schedule unless it was something meaningful. I suspected there was more to her words than she let on.

Later, when I asked again, pressing her gently, she finally said, "There has been a wish in my heart for a long time, my dear. Only you can fulfill it."

Her words surprised me. How could my mother, who had fulfilled every wish of mine, have an unfulfilled wish herself? I eagerly urged her to share it, promising I would do whatever it took to make it come true.

"My life's journey has been filled with twists and turns," she began. "This house, built by your father, has been my sanctuary. But as time moves forward, I sense that my journey may soon reach its end. Before that day comes, I want to prepare.

Here's my wish: Let's sell this house. I don't need such a big place anymore. A simple, small room would suffice for me to live peacefully for the rest of my days. You can use the money for your business, your dreams, or however you see fit. There's no need to account for it to me. If you have time, help me make the arrangements."

Her words shocked me. Could this truly be my mother speaking? It felt unlike her—a woman so deeply spiritual and wise, always seeing life beyond the material. Her request seemed almost out of place, and I realized she must have deeper intentions. I decided to reflect on it before responding.

After some time, I returned to her with my answer.

"Mom, I've thought about your words carefully. Now, please hear me out.

This isn't just a house; it's a sanctuary of love. It's a sacred temple, the place where you raised me and filled my life with meaning. This home is no less than a divine abode to me. Selling it would feel like parting with a piece of my soul.

After you, I want this house to remain a testament to the love and memories that you and Dad built here. I will visit it often, remembering both of you and feeling your presence in its walls. The garden should always bloom with flowers that spread their fragrance. The pond behind the house should always host playful little fish, kissing its shores. Birds should continue to sing in the trees, filling this space with their melodies. Even the cows grazing nearby, their calves frolicking, should add life to this place.

This house must always stand as a sanctuary for love and memories. The money from selling it could never bring me the joy this home provides. After me, my children will also ensure its preservation. Please forgive me, Mom, but I cannot fulfill this wish of yours."

Tears welled up in her eyes. She held my hands, her voice trembling with emotion but unable to speak. Her silence told me she understood.

Eventually, she nodded in agreement. Her smile conveyed acceptance, and I realized she had tested me with this wish. It was her way of confirming whether I understood the true value of this home.

In that moment, my mother's heart found peace, and mine soared like a bird, filled with joy. Her love, her wisdom, and her gentle test had left me with an enduring lesson: my mother's only true wish was for me to honor the values she had instilled in me.

As I prepared to leave, the house seemed to glow brighter, as if the very walls were rejoicing in our shared love and understanding.

The Unexpected Guest

There's a remarkable moment from my life's journey that I keep reminiscing about—a cherished memory from my 50th birthday. It was a day that left an indelible mark on me.

My children were settled abroad, and due to circumstances, my wife had gone to stay with them for some time. My mother, my constant source of blessings, was far away. Yet, as she always did, she sent me her heartfelt wishes for the day.

The weather outside was stormy, with relentless winds and heavy rain. Given the situation, I had invited only a few close friends from nearby to celebrate the occasion. The preparations were complete, and I waited eagerly for my friends to arrive.

The storm intensified, with the wind howling louder and the rain lashing harder. I secured all the windows and doors and sat down, resigned to spending the evening alone. Then, unexpectedly, the electricity went out. The lights flickered and died, plunging the house into darkness. The atmosphere felt ominous. A sense of unease crept in as I realized that no one would be able to make it in this weather.

With great effort, I lit a candle and sat quietly, the dim glow casting shadows around me. The storm outside seemed relentless, and it became clear that even my nearest friends couldn't brave the weather.

This was a stark contrast to the joyous celebrations of my past birthdays, which were always filled with family, friends, and warmth. Tonight, the solitude weighed heavily on me, and the storm mirrored the turmoil in my heart. As the candle melted away and the clock edged toward midnight, I began to accept the reality: I was alone.

Then, unexpectedly, I heard a knock at the door. My heart leapt with joy. Could it be a friend, braving the storm to be with me? The thought filled me with hope. I rushed to the door, grateful for such loyal companionship.

Opening the door, I was met with a gust of cold wind and pouring rain. The dim candlelight made it hard to see the visitor clearly. I strained to recognize the figure. The candle extinguished in the wind, plunging everything into darkness.

I felt a pair of soft, cold, trembling hands touch my face. Those hands moved gently to my cheeks, brushing away the wetness, and then to my hair, tidying it with love. Those hands were familiar—hands that had comforted me countless times, hands that had always given me warmth and affection.

It was her. It was my mother.

"Mother? Is it really you? Have you come all this way, through this storm, just to bless me on my birthday?" My voice trembled, my words faltering as my emotions overwhelmed me.

Without saying much, she simply pulled me close, her touch as soothing as ever. I knelt before her in the darkness, laying my head at her feet. Her hands rested gently on my head, and her voice, soft but clear amidst the storm's roar, spoke words that filled the room with light.

"Happy birthday, my child. May you live a long, fulfilling life."

Even in the midst of a storm, my mother's love had found its way to me

Heart Felt Manifestations

One day, a renowned spiritual guru visited our college. He was known for his profound teachings, his ability to correct one's flaws, and his skill in shaping personalities. Our professors introduced him with great reverence, seating him in an honored chair and requesting him to address us.

The guru spoke at length, sharing remarkable insights, offering inspiration, and filling us with renewed energy. He eloquently described the power and greatness of the Divine and captivated us with his depiction of the wondrous deeds of God. In the end, he began asking questions to gauge our understanding.

Turning to me, he asked, "Who is the creator of this universe, my child?"

Without hesitation, I replied, "My mother and father."

Everyone burst into laughter, but the guru raised his hand to quiet them.

"The Creator is God, my child," he corrected me gently.

I disagreed. "No, Master. It is our mother and father who are the true creators. Without them, even God would not exist. Without them, there would be no birth. It is the union of feminine and masculine energies that creates life."

The room fell silent. The guru listened intently as I elaborated, explaining what my mother had taught me:

"It is through the union of these energies that all life forms—be they insects, animals, birds, plants, or humans—come into existence. My mother taught me that the vital force within us is the Divine itself. The breath we inhale and exhale carries the essence of God. The great scriptures are the distilled essence of life experiences, and those who wrote them were simply sharing their wisdom gained through life."

The guru's curiosity deepened. "What else did your mother teach you? Come closer and share with us."

Encouraged, I walked to the stage and began speaking by his side.

"My mother asked me if we could live as freely as the lion, without being enslaved by anything or anyone. Can we bear responsibilities like the elephant? Can we soar to great heights like the eagle? Can we sing as sweetly as the cuckoo? Can we bloom like the lotus, radiating pure joy? Can we, like the silkworm, spin something of beauty from within? Can we, like the ant, work tirelessly? And finally, can we live with the unwavering loyalty of a dog?"

I paused, my words echoing in the silence. Looking around, I saw that everyone was motionless, staring at me as if entranced. I turned to the guru, whose calm expression urged me to continue.

"She also warned me to avoid certain traits: not to emulate the tiger's cruelty, the snake's venom, the jackal's deceit, the pig's filth, or the snail's sluggishness."

Before I could proceed further, the guru interjected. "Does this mean that humans have nothing to teach us? Are they worthless compared to animals?"

I responded, "Not at all, Master. Humans learn the most from their mothers. A person who embodies a mother's love becomes a Rama. One who declares her way of life as righteousness becomes a Krishna. One who shares her compassion with the world becomes a Christ. And one who follows her peace and patience becomes a Buddha. These are lessons I learned from observing my mother."

The guru's face lit up with admiration. "Where is this extraordinary mother of yours? I would like to meet her."

I smiled and replied, "Mother is not just my mother, Master. She is the 'Universal Mother.' She resides in every breath we take, in the life force within us, in the beat of our hearts. She taught us how to walk, how to speak, how to think. Everything we are is shaped by her. She is the essence within us, and we are but manifestations of her."

The room erupted in applause, and I felt a profound sense of joy and pride.

The guru's eyes glistened with emotion as he said, "I must meet your mother. Will you take me to her?"

His words, filled with heartfelt sincerity, sent shivers down my spine.

—·—·—●—·—·—

Sanctuary of Peace

A friend of mine often sought solace in mountain caves, believing that true peace of mind could only be achieved by distancing oneself from family troubles and meditating in solitude. However, my life experiences taught me a vastly different truth: peace of mind thrives in the company of loved ones, especially family. This conviction was shaped by the countless moments I shared with my mother, whose wisdom consistently reaffirmed that true tranquility resides in familial bonds, not in isolation.

My mother's presence was a beacon in my life, molding it in miraculous ways. Her every word was a lesson, imbued with love and compassion. These teachings left an indelible mark on me, proving time and again that peace is a state of mind, not a product of one's surroundings. She often said, "No one can find peace by running away. True peace lies in living among people, being one with them, and remaining undisturbed by external pressures."

This principle guided my life. When external pressures overwhelmed me, I found relief at home, where my mother's presence and wisdom provided clarity. Her teachings emphasized that peace of mind should never come at the expense of one's responsibilities.

My childhood and adolescence unfolded at my mother's feet, filled with joy and comfort. Her presence was the answer to all my problems, and the lessons she imparted in those formative years laid the foundation for my thoughts and beliefs today. They continue to shield me from the uncertainties of tomorrow.

Once, I visited a temple with friends. A priest offered me a pinch of vermilion, saying, "You don't have a mark on your forehead. Take this and apply it."

I declined politely. "I already bear a sacred mark on my forehead," I said.

He insisted, "There's no mark visible. Let me give you this."

I replied, "The dust of my mother's feet adorns my forehead, and that is more sacred to me than any vermilion."

My words did not sit well with the priest, and he declared me unworthy of entering the temple. Undeterred, I returned home with a joyful heart, basking in the divine presence of my mother.

For as long as I can remember, it has been my habit to touch my mother's feet and place my hands on my face before stepping out of the house. This simple act, imbued with reverence, has always brought me countless successes. It's not merely a ritual but a source of profound faith and fortune.

My mother always taught me that artificial adornments do not enhance beauty; living in perpetual joy is the essence of true beauty. She believed that nothing is more valuable than the wealth of happiness.

Even the most breathtaking natural wonders cannot match the joy found in the shadow of a mother's love. My mother's smile is a shower of affection, her words a pathway lined with flowers, and her gaze a tender caress of kindness. Her face radiates the cool, comforting glow of countless moons, and her voice resonates like a sublime melody, preceding the anthems of success. Her heart is a sacred temple, and her feet a sanctuary offering eternal rest.

How, then, can lifeless mountains or caves provide the peace that a mother's presence effortlessly bestows? Even in the solitude of a mountain cave, the unresolved challenges of daily life will echo in the chambers of one's heart. But when sitting silently at a mother's feet, those challenges dissipate, leaving only the serene rhythm of one's heartbeat.

This is why my friend's pursuit of peace in distant caves didn't sit well with me. I urged him to return home.

"Go to your mother," I said. "Seek refuge at her feet. She is the only one who can grant you true peace. For your happiness, she sacrifices her own and prays to the Divine with more devotion than anyone else ever could. Go and find your peace in her presence."

Moved by my words and filled with love for his mother, my friend left for home. As I watched him walk away, I, too, turned back with joy in my heart, cherishing the thought of my own mother.

———•———

The Woman Within Him

I had a distant relative, about my age, who tragically lost his mother at a young age. One day, as I sat alone, my thoughts drifted to him, and an overwhelming sense of pity filled my heart. How was he growing up without a mother? Who was feeding him, comforting him in difficult times, wiping away his tears, and guiding him with wisdom? Who was loving him like a mother, holding his hand, and walking beside him? The thought of his motherless existence seemed unbearably bleak.

I shared my concern with my mother. She smiled gently and said, "You're overthinking this. The divine provides for everyone. Don't worry; he must be happy."

But her words didn't satisfy me. To me, a house without a mother was like a temple without a deity—empty and lifeless.

Determined to see for myself, I decided to visit him. I wanted to comfort him, offer him support, and let him know he was not alone. With these thoughts, I set off for his village.

When I arrived at his home, he greeted me warmly and embraced me with joy. What surprised me, however, was his demeanor—he radiated happiness. Contrary to my expectations, he appeared content and at peace, his face glowing with satisfaction. His cheerful disposition puzzled me.

The house exuded a tender care that only a woman, a mother, could provide. My curiosity intensified. I had to know what was happening. Without hesitation, I asked him, "Your father must have remarried, right? You have a stepmother now, and she has brought joy and order to this home. Isn't that why you're so happy?"

He shook his head firmly. I was taken aback.

"Then you must be in love. Your father must have blessed your relationship, and it is your beloved who brings light to this house. Is that it?"

Again, he shook his head. "No," he said. "There is no woman in this house. The light you see comes from my father. It is his love and care that fills this home. The happiness you see in me comes from seeing him."

His words astonished me. How could this be possible? I asked him to explain, and what he said next revealed profound truths I had never considered.

"I never once wished for a mother or felt the need for a woman's presence in this home. My father made sure I never felt that void. He has been everything to me—a mother, a brother, a friend.

Every morning, he wakes me with a kiss on my forehead. He is always ready before I even express my needs. He sees my nourishment and protection as his sacred duties. He comforts me in sorrow, shines as a beacon of hope in despair, walks beside me as a companion, and opens his heart as a vast empire of love for me to dwell in. He lives for me, dedicating himself entirely to my happiness, while inspiring me to live my life for him. When I'm weary, he sits beside me, sings me lullabies, and soothes me to sleep. My father embodies all the qualities of a mother. I feel no lack because he has shown me the essence of motherhood through his actions. My gratitude for him overflows in every fiber of my being."

I was awestruck by his words. Leaving his divine home, I returned to mine with a deep sense of enlightenment. I narrated the entire incident to my mother, who listened intently. Her response filled me with even more joy.

"In every man lies a part of a woman, and in every woman, a part of a man. A mother's spirit resides in a father, and a father's strength resides in a mother. In a true husband, the soul of his wife lives, and in a true wife, the soul of her husband thrives. Children raised in such homes are truly fortunate; they lack nothing. His father is a wise man. It is only the ignorant who seek external support, leaving their children to suffer like orphans. This is an eternal and universal truth."

My mother's words echoed the profound realization I had witnessed. In that moment, I understood the divinity of love and the boundless strength it holds, transcending roles and fulfilling lives.

Love Triumphs

One day, a small argument with my friend escalated into a heated quarrel, and before I knew it, he raised his hand against me. The confrontation left me bruised, and I ran home, hurt both physically and emotionally.

When my mother saw me, her face turned pale with worry. "Take me to your friend," she said firmly. I could sense the anger in her voice. I knew that my mother, who had the strength of a goddess when it came to protecting me, was ready to confront anyone.

Holding her hand, I led her to my friend's house. When my friend saw us approaching, he panicked and hid inside. His parents, sensing trouble, came out and started apologizing profusely, holding my mother's hand and asking for forgiveness.

My mother's stern expression didn't soften. Her silence was loud with disapproval. It was clear she hadn't forgiven them yet. "Bring your son to me," she said. Her tone was resolute, leaving no room for argument. Though hesitant, they brought my friend out and handed him over to my mother, unsure of what was to come.

But instead of scolding him, my mother did something unexpected. She took him to our home, leaving everyone stunned. Once inside, she let go of my hand and walked toward him. To my utter amazement, she pulled him into a warm embrace. She kissed his forehead and gently patted his back. Her actions bewildered me. I had expected her to reprimand him harshly, but here she was, showering him with affection.

"Mother, what are you doing? You haven't even treated my wounds, yet you're comforting him!" I asked, unable to contain my confusion.

My mother smiled and said, "Your body is wounded, but his heart is scarred. Your injuries will heal in time, but his pain needs immediate attention, or it will fester and destroy him."

Her words didn't make sense to me at first. She then made us sit side by side on the couch, so close that our shoulders touched. Smiling, she asked, "How does it feel to sit like this?"

"Warm," we both replied instinctively.

"Anger and hatred are like fire," she said. "They burn the body and torment the soul. Love, on the other hand, is like a soft flower, like soothing rain. It cools the body and fills the mind with joy. When you strike with a stone, it hurts. But when you strike with a bouquet of flowers, it soothes. You are young and impressionable, like fertile soil. Whatever seeds are planted now will grow into towering trees. Anger is the greatest enemy, while love is the most precious treasure. Enmity is a curse; friendship is a divine gift. Always conquer hatred with love and live a life of friendship.

Hatred and anger will eventually die out like flames that turn to ash. But enmity can only be erased by love. If people learned this, would wars, conflicts, and violence still exist? The world would become a haven of peace, with the banner of love flying high.

Fight with flowers. Shatter hardness with kindness, compassion, and empathy. When you shower love, even stones turn into sculptures. You are the torchbearers of tomorrow. Be the light that guides the world into a better future."

My friend, deeply moved by her words, broke down in tears. He hugged me tightly and apologized, transforming from an adversary into a true friend.

His parents, who had come searching for him in panic, arrived at our house and stood at the door, watching in awe as my mother's words worked their magic. They bowed to her with immense gratitude, saying, "This is what it means to touch someone's heart and transform them."

My mother responded humbly, "These words were not just for your son; they are meant for my child too."

And she was right. Her wisdom applied to everyone. If the world thought and acted like my mother, it would indeed become one harmonious family.

The Garden of Joy

That day was my father's birthday. Determined to gift him something special, I had saved up my money and bought a thoughtful present. I eagerly planned to give it to him the moment he woke up. However, as usual, my father had already left for work by the time I got up. I stayed home, waiting for him to return.

Curious about what my mother might have prepared for my father, I asked her, "What gift did you get for Dad?"

She smiled and replied, "I didn't buy anything."

She went on with her day as though it was just another ordinary one, tidying up the house. I couldn't help but feel perplexed. "Poor Dad! He'll be disappointed," I thought. In that moment, I felt a little superior, proud of the gift I had prepared for him.

I decided to observe her. She transformed the house with meticulous care, making every corner shine. She moved about with joy, as if she were preparing for a grand celebration. She went out to the yard, fed the cattle, whispered to them lovingly, and scattered grains for the birds, chatting with them as if they understood her. She touched the flowers gently, her face lighting up as if she shared their bloom. By the pond, she set up a comfortable chair, petted the fish as if they were children, and released them back into the water tenderly.

After a refreshing bath, she wore clean, crisp clothes and began cooking in the kitchen. The aroma of her cooking filled the house, spreading a festive vibe. Finally, she sat on the front porch, waiting for my father with a peaceful smile.

Her actions puzzled me further. How could a wife not buy her husband a gift on his birthday? I had never seen my parents exchange gifts, but today, being home all day, I couldn't stop wondering.

Feeling proud of my gift, I also waited eagerly for my father.

When he arrived, I rushed to greet him with a happy "Happy Birthday!" and handed him my present. His face lit up as he opened it, and he pulled me into a warm hug, kissing my forehead. He excitedly showed the gift to my mother, beaming like a child. She praised me with joy in her eyes. Seeing their happiness filled me with a deep sense of satisfaction.

The house seemed to hum with positivity. My father stepped outside onto the porch, took a deep breath, and looked around.

"Is this a house or a divine temple?" he exclaimed.

My mother smiled, and I silently agreed.

Father walked to the yard, and I followed him. The cattle ran up to him affectionately, nudging him as if to wish him. He stroked them gently, spending a moment in their company. Then he moved to the flower garden, where the blossoms swayed as though bowing to greet him. Birds perched in their nests burst into a chorus of songs that sounded like birthday melodies.

At the pond, he sat in the chair my mother had prepared. The fish leapt joyfully in and out of the water, performing an enchanting dance. Sunlight filtered through the trees, casting warm, golden rays, while the cool breeze gently caressed the surroundings.

It felt as though nature itself was celebrating my father's birthday.

Later, we feasted on the delicious dishes my mother had prepared. Watching my father revel in joy and contentment, I realized that my mother had gifted him the most priceless present—a home transformed into paradise. She was a goddess of love and care, orchestrating everything with devotion and grace.

The entire house resonated with happiness that day. It felt as though three celestial stars had descended to our home, filling it with radiant light and boundless bliss. Our house wasn't just a home; it was a sanctuary of joy.

In truth, our house is always a haven of happiness. That's why my father eagerly returns home every day. My mother radiates joy like a perpetual lamp, and my parents together are the beacons of light that fill my life with energy and hope. Every day feels like a birthday celebration in our home.

I often remember my mother's profound words: "Every moment we breathe is a gift, and every breath is a new birthday."

A Shower of Smiles

One day, my wife asked me an intriguing question:

"Why do people respect your words so much? How do you manage to respond with a smile, even in the most serious situations?"

Until she asked, I hadn't thought about it much. It was true—I always seemed to get a favorable response from people. Even those who approached me with intense arguments would eventually calm down in the warmth of my smile. My friends used to joke that even a person wielding a sword would lower it upon seeing me smile.

In business meetings, I was always the one chosen for negotiations, and I almost always returned victorious. I couldn't recall having any enemies; if I did, they never revealed themselves.

Elders and wise people often praised me, saying that my tone carried simplicity and love, like a gentle rain. Their compliments filled me with pride, even without garlands or applause.

But I never consciously trained myself to be this way. I had no lessons in personality development, never read books on psychology, nor listened to motivational speeches. Everything I embodied was a reflection of my mother's compassion. Her teachings, especially one core principle, had shaped me deeply:

"Everyone's argument makes sense to them. To bring them to your way of thinking, love is the only path."

Her wisdom became my mantra, and her gentleness became my shield. People often remarked, "You envelop us in a rain of smiles. We can't resist you." Once, a foreign delegate even said this to me, a compliment I recall with fondness.

(The Special Day)

The day my wife asked me that question was after a particular event. We had attended a meeting with many representatives, most of whom already knew me. Naturally, I received a warm and friendly reception.

During the meeting, I spoke, and the response was overwhelming. My words resonated with the crowd, and they showered me with compliments. On our way back home, my wife teased me.

"I'm starting to get jealous of you," she said, laughing.

I chuckled, thinking she was joking, but then she added, "One of your friends said something interesting today. He said, 'There's a woman hidden in you. That's why even men are drawn to you.'"

She smiled playfully, but her words lingered. Later that night, they came back to me.

(A Journey of Reflection)

Curious and slightly amused, I went to my room and stood before the mirror. I looked at my face, trying to see what others saw. My eyes, my nose, my lips, my cheeks—they all seemed soft, almost delicate. I wasn't sure if I felt embarrassed or proud.

"Am I really this handsome?" I mused, half-jokingly, and continued to examine myself.

As I stared, a strange sense of familiarity dawned on me. This wasn't just my face—it felt like I was looking at someone else's reflection. A face filled with smiles, eyes brimming with moonlight, radiating kindness and compassion.

And then it hit me. This was *her* face. My mother's face.

But there was something more. Something different. I kept looking, and then I saw it—a blend, a perfect harmony. My nose, sharp and pointed, resembled my father's. My soft, rosy cheeks were my mother's. My wavy hair came from my father, but my arched eyebrows were undoubtedly hers.

(An Extraordinary Union)

I realized that my appearance, my demeanor, and my essence were the result of an extraordinary union. Like nectar in a flower, like fragrance in the air, like sweetness in a melody, I was the harmonious outcome of their beautiful blend.

Yes, I was the fruit of their love, a living testament to their joy-filled union. I was a part of both of them, carrying their essence in every fiber of my being.

I whispered to myself with gratitude:

"I am blessed, Mother. I am blessed, Father."

Their legacy lives on in me, and for that, I am eternally grateful.

—·—·—●—·—·—

The Everlasting Wealth

One day, my mother and I had an extraordinary conversation—a profound exchange that reshaped my understanding of life and its ultimate purpose. That day, I truly realized that my mother was not just a parent but a repository of wisdom, a teacher who unveiled universal truths and guided me toward clarity.

During our conversation, I casually brought up a close friend of mine.

"He's incredibly wealthy, Mother. Grand buildings, luxurious cars, countless employees—there's nothing he lacks," I said with admiration.

Mother's response startled me.

"Have you ever observed his bedroom? Does he sleep peacefully? Does he breathe easily while he sleeps?"

I had no answer. Her words made me pause, but I still felt compelled to defend my friend's greatness, convinced that Mother was not fully grasping the magnitude of his success. Determined, I continued.

"But, Mother, he is incredibly strong and powerful. Ordinary people cannot challenge him."

"Is his mind as strong as his body? Or is it as soft as a flower? Can he withstand hardships?"

I tried another approach.

"He is extremely well-educated. I doubt anyone has higher qualifications than him."

"Is that so? Does he hold a degree in understanding the essence of life? Has he touched the boundaries of wisdom? Does he read not just books but also people and their hearts?"

I was persistent.

"He has immense authority, Mother. People bow before him."

"Do they bow out of respect or fear? Does he have genuine well-wishers, or are there hidden enemies around him? Have you ever tried to find out?"

"He has a large family, Mother. His home is always bustling with relatives and activity."

"Are they there for him? Would they stand by him in both prosperity and adversity?"

I tried tirelessly to glorify my friend, but Mother skillfully countered every argument with incisive questions that left me speechless. Feeling defeated, I quietly walked away.

(The Revelation)

Alone in my thoughts, I pondered Mother's words. Slowly, the layers of my ignorance peeled away, and profound truths began to emerge. It was as if her questions themselves held the answers. That day, I understood what true wealth meant and who could truly be considered rich in this world.

Mother's words were not just guidance; they were revelations. Her questions were not meant to criticize but to teach, and in their simplicity lay the deepest wisdom.

"Peaceful sleep is the greatest blessing," I realized.

"No matter how much wealth one has, it's meaningless without rest. A beggar sleeping under a tree, free of worries, is far more fortunate than a wealthy man troubled by sleepless nights."

"Physical strength fades with time," I thought, "but mental resilience grows stronger with life's experiences. It is the foundation of true stability and courage."

"Education is confined to books," I reflected, "but wisdom knows no bounds. The universe is a classroom, and life itself is the teacher."

"Power instills fear," I realized. "Admiration, on the other hand, fosters love. Authority is temporary and breeds enemies, while genuine affection draws friends closer."

Mother's questions had led me to these revelations. Her wisdom transcended ordinary teachings, shaping my perspective and sharpening my understanding.

(The Ultimate Teacher)

I returned to Mother, humbled and enlightened.

"Mother," I said, "you are the greatest teacher I could ever have. Your words hold more meaning than their surface suggests. You've taught me to see beyond the obvious, to seek the deeper truths hidden in life."

Mother smiled, her eyes radiating warmth.

"True wealth, my child, is not in what you possess but in how you live. Peace, wisdom, resilience, and love—these are the treasures that last forever."

Her words stayed with me, echoing in my mind and heart. In that moment, I saw her not just as my mother but as the ultimate teacher, guiding me toward the wealth that truly matters.

—·—·—●—·—·—

The Inner Soul

Sleep evades me. Hunger feels like a distant memory. My heart grows heavy, and the light in my life seems to dim. A burden I cannot share with anyone weighs down on me. If only I could find solace under a comforting shade, a place to rest my troubled soul. But who can be that solace? Whose shadow can I seek to lighten my heart?

Perhaps my mother. But why trouble her with my burdens? Yet, simply being near her might ease the weight on my mind. Without burdening her, I thought, I could still find relief. With this hope, I set out to see her.

This event happened nearly forty years ago. Recalling it now brings back vivid memories of a transformative moment with my mother.

When I reached her, she was overjoyed to see me. As always, she sat beside me, placed her hand on mine, and began asking about my well-being, my work, my life. She disappeared into the kitchen, intent on preparing something to fill my stomach.

She was as joyous as a child, her face glowing with happiness. Just being in her presence felt like stepping into a haven, full of moonlight, a refreshing breeze in the scorching heat. My heavy heart started to feel lighter, and my mind began to find its rhythm again.

But I had resolved not to trouble her with my difficulties. Instead, I became a storyteller, weaving tales of a perfect life—of restful nights, a smooth career, and a carefree existence. I wanted her to believe I had come to share my happiness, not my troubles.

In truth, I was deeply distressed. The company where I worked was drowning in financial turmoil. For six months, salaries had gone unpaid, and hundreds of employees, myself included, had lost their jobs. The economic crisis made finding another job nearly impossible. Supporting my family seemed like an insurmountable challenge.

I had come to my mother, hoping her presence would give me a fresh perspective and the strength to face my troubles.

During my time with her, she filled my days with love, care, and comfort. She ensured I felt no lack and treated me with endless affection. Only when I felt somewhat unburdened did I tell her, "Mother, I will leave tomorrow."

She agreed without question, never asking why or where. That night, we sat together under the moonlit sky in the courtyard. The breeze was gentle, the ripples in the pond made soft sounds, and the trees swayed gracefully in the wind.

Breaking the silence, she asked, "Don't the waves in the pond ever tire? Doesn't the wind ever rest? Don't the fragrances in the garden ever fade? And doesn't the moonlight's coolness ever wane?"

Her questions were beautiful, yet profound. I realized she was about to speak something significant. So, I sat quietly, listening.

"I love you dearly, my child—more than my own life. But alongside you, I also admire certain other things. I love the rivers that flow tirelessly. I adore the waves that rise and fall in the vast oceans. I respect the mountains that stand unyielding through storms. I cherish the eagle that soars above the clouds with unmatched confidence. I marvel at the spider that patiently rebuilds its web despite countless falls. And I admire the ant that labors endlessly without rest."

Her words sent chills down my spine. Did she know about my struggles? Had she discerned the lies I had told to shield her from worry?

I realized my foolishness. A child cannot deceive a mother who sees and feels everything. I laid my head at her feet, overwhelmed with humility.

"How did you know?" I asked her.

"Your words and your body both carry vibrations, my child. They told me everything," she said softly.

In that moment, I saw her not just as a mother but as a wise psychologist, a healer of hearts.

"I will fight, Mother. I will work hard. I will rise again, stronger than before. I will turn my lies into truths and earn your pride. Bless me," I said, once again bowing at her feet.

She gently placed her hands on my head, her touch filling me with a sense of purpose. In her embrace, I found new strength, renewed energy, and a reminder of my own resilience. She awakened the dormant spirit within me, helping me recognize my inner self.

That night, under the moonlit sky, my mother rekindled my will to fight. She didn't just lighten my burden; she transformed it into the courage I needed to face the challenges ahead.

A Walk, A Way of Life

At our school, a new teacher joined. The first time he entered our class, we all burst into laughter. His leg was crooked, and he walked with a limp, lifting each foot high as he stepped into the room. We had never seen such a teacher before, and his walk appeared strange to us. It amused us so much that it reminded us of a limping crow that often wandered into our yard. We decided to call him "Kunti Master" (the limping teacher), a nickname that quickly spread among all the children at school.

The surprising part was that he didn't seem offended. Instead, he smiled and responded warmly, saying, "Yes, I limp, don't I?" Occasionally, he would even perform a funny dance with his limp, making us laugh. His humor kept us engaged and ensured no one skipped school.

Over time, "Kunti Master" became his identity, even outside the school. People in the village also began referring to him by this name, and he responded with the same cheerful acceptance.

One day, while studying in my room, an odd thought crossed my mind. I decided to mimic our teacher's limp as I read my lessons. Walking like him, pretending to stumble, and even imitating his dance, I entertained myself and laughed alone. It became a game that I thoroughly enjoyed.

Unbeknownst to me, my mother was watching through the window. Seeing her, I decided to amplify my antics, hoping to amuse her too.

"You're a great actor, my child," she said with a smile. "But remember, always be yourself. It's getting late—go to bed now."

Her words, calling me a good actor, filled me with pride. That night, I fell asleep, brimming with satisfaction.

The next day, at school, I boasted to my friends about my imitation skills, enjoying their laughter and praise. It was a joyous day. After school, I eagerly returned home, but the scene awaiting me stopped me in my tracks.

My mother lay on the bed, with my father sitting beside her, tending to her needs. Panic surged through me as I ran to her side.

"What happened?" I asked, my voice trembling.

"She slipped in the kitchen and fell," my father replied, his face somber.

My mother smiled faintly at me, but it was a heavy, weary smile. Seeing her like that, I broke down and wept.

"What now?" I asked, desperate for reassurance.

"Her leg is fractured. She won't be able to walk for some time," my father said.

The words struck me like a thunderbolt. The mother who moved with such grace, who danced like a swan, whose steps were as lively as a fawn's—now she couldn't walk?

I closed my eyes, unable to bear the thought. In my mind's eye, I saw her limping like our teacher. The image haunted me. I clung to her, sobbing uncontrollably.

Gently stroking my head, my mother broke the silence.

"Is this how you handle a little hardship, my child? You're distraught seeing me temporarily unable to walk. But tell me, your teacher, who walks with a limp every day, has brought you joy.

Did you ever stop to think about the challenges he faces? Did his difficulty become your amusement?

A person's gait is less important than their way of life. It's okay if one's leg falters, but never let your heart or conscience stumble.

Kindness, compassion, and love are treasures I've tried to instill in you. Don't let them fade. I slipped because I was worried that my teachings were failing to guide you.

Never mock anyone, my dear. Instead, admire, love, and respect them. I want to see virtues take root in you—not vices. My condition doesn't matter, but I fear for the person you may become. Don't let your way of life limp, my child."

Her words pierced my heart and opened my eyes. That day, a new awareness dawned upon me. I felt as if a sleeping part of my soul had awakened.

(The next morning) Instantly, I rushed to school and sought out my teacher. As he prepared to leave, I ran up to him. Smiling, he greeted me warmly. But I didn't stop there. I fell to my knees and touched both his feet, tears streaming down my face.

"Please forgive me," I said, my voice choked with emotion.

He lifted me up gently, embraced me, and blessed me with all his heart.

Though he worked at our school for only two years before being transferred, his impact on my life was profound. He left an indelible mark, shaping me into the person I am today. To me, he was more than a teacher—he was like a second mother, guiding me with love and wisdom.

Even today, he occasionally reaches out, checking on my well-being and celebrating my successes from afar. Through him, I learned the true essence of beauty—not in appearances, but in strength, kindness, and the way we walk through life.

The Enchantment of Wisdom

One day, I helped a beggar. On another, I gave charity to a destitute person. I secured a job for an unemployed youth. Over time, I extended support in countless ways to both friends and strangers. I expected my help to bring them joy, peace, and fulfillment. I believed I had achieved immense satisfaction by brightening their lives.

But to my surprise, their joy was short-lived. Before long, they reverted to their struggles and discontent, weighed down by the burdens of life. The happiness I thought I had given them seemed to dissolve. Why was this happening? Where did my efforts and their happiness go?

My sense of fulfillment turned into dissatisfaction. Could it be possible that my intention to spread joy brought unintended consequences?

I pondered deeply over this. I read books, studied the lives of many, and sought wisdom from elders. Gradually, I realized a profound truth: human existence is caught in an endless cycle of unfulfilled desires, hovering between fleeting joys and life's inevitable end.

A person can be made happy for a moment, but no human can grant another permanent happiness. This revelation stirred a new curiosity within me: If joy is fleeting, how can it be made enduring? What leads humanity to eternal bliss?

I discussed this question with friends and wise individuals. Many dismissed the idea of eternal happiness, claiming it was an illusion. They argued that, like day and night, joy and sorrow are complementary and inseparable.

But I wasn't convinced. I believed in the existence of eternal happiness. If such a concept did not exist, why would humanity strive for it so relentlessly? The very word "happiness" suggests it has an ultimate, enduring form.

Observing life, I saw people constantly chasing more—whether it was wealth, knowledge, or fulfilling one desire after another. The more they achieved, the more they longed for. This endless pursuit left them exhausted, disillusioned, and often despairing.

I began to question: When will this cycle end? Is there a solution, a mantra (chant) that can bring true contentment? Who could enlighten me with the answers?

I knew there was only one person who could—my mother. Over the years, I had turned to her for insights into life's most complex questions. She was the embodiment of joy, radiating contentment in every moment. Her serene face shone with peace, even in her sleep.

I went to her with reverence, sat at her feet, and asked her to guide me.

"My dear," she said after listening patiently, "I am but a simple woman. I haven't studied scriptures or learned philosophies. I'm an ordinary mother, living an ordinary life. What wisdom could I possibly offer you?"

"Mother," I pleaded, "your life itself is the answer I seek. How do you live so contentedly? What worries you? What eases your mind? Just share your way of life with me."

She sat in silence for a moment, and then began to speak, her voice calm and profound:

"Life, my child, is a great illusion created by the divine. It is a boundless ocean, its depths unfathomable. To try to unravel all its mysteries is sheer folly. Wanting to plumb its depths is the root of all suffering.

People overlook the joy before them, chasing shadows and illusions of happiness elsewhere. Not knowing what true joy is, humans are less fortunate than animals, who live in complete harmony with nature. Humans, despite their intellect, are often the greatest fools.

Joy, my dear, is a divine light that resides within us. Instead of nurturing it, people cover it with veils of desires and wander in darkness, searching for light outside themselves.

Happiness is of the mind. It must be experienced within. External pleasures may momentarily delight, but like mirages, they disappear as we approach. The real sorrow lies in neglecting what we have and yearning for what we don't.

You asked how I live my life. Let me tell you:

- I find immense joy in the presence of your father. Whether he is by my side or far away, I live in his company or in his memories.

- I pray with unwavering faith for the well-being of my children.

- I only do what is necessary and stay away from forbidden or harmful actions.

- love everyone and treat myself as my greatest asset.

- I help without expecting anything in return.

- Every breath I take, I consider it a blessing—a treasure of wealth beyond measure.

That is all, my son."

Her words enveloped me like a gentle breeze, dispelling the darkness clouding my mind. In her simple, unassuming manner, she had revealed profound truths. My mother wasn't just a mother—she was a fountain of wisdom, an embodiment of divine grace.

As I sat there in awe, I realized why she was always joyful. Her contentment wasn't tied to external factors. It stemmed from within—a timeless lesson she had now passed on to me.

The Undefeated Love

We were on our return journey from a distant place. My friend and I were traveling in a car, passing through a quaint village.

As we entered the heart of the village, we noticed a large crowd gathered in the middle of the street. Thinking that perhaps an accident or some emergency had occurred, we stopped nearby to offer assistance. My friend stepped out of the car to investigate, while I waited, curious and concerned.

A few moments later, he returned to the car, laughing. "What happened?" I asked.

"It's nothing serious," he said. "They're hosting a rooster fight."

"A rooster fight? What's that?"

"It's a popular rural sport," he explained. "Two roosters are armed with blades tied to their legs and put in an arena to fight. One emerges victorious, while the other often dies. People bet on the outcome. The winning rooster survives, and its owner earns money, while the losing rooster's fate seals the owner's loss."

I listened in silence, my mind pondering this grim spectacle. "It's a covert form of war," I remarked. My friend nodded in agreement.

I have always held a distaste for competitions where one's gain is another's loss. These battles—be it in games or life—often breed pride in the victor and humiliation in the defeated. The victor celebrates while the loser hangs their head in shame. Such contests can erode goodwill, foster animosity, and extinguish the spirit of camaraderie.

"Have you ever seen a game where both the winner and loser experience joy?" I asked my friend.

"That's impossible!" he exclaimed. "How can the defeated ever find joy in losing? That doesn't happen in this world."

"Oh, but it does," I replied with a smile. "There exists an extraordinary game, one that we all witness but often fail to notice."

His curiosity piqued, he asked, "Really? A game like that? Tell me about it!"

I began to explain:

"This game is called life. And the most enchanting match within it is played by two opponents: Mother and Father. Their shared goal is singular—to envelop their child in love and joy.

The father plays with unyielding dedication, investing his sweat and toil as his currency. His aim is to nurture his child with discipline and guidance, ensuring a brighter future. Every small achievement of his child, every step that surpasses his own, becomes his greatest triumph. For this, he labors tirelessly, taking pride in building a golden path for his child.

On the other side is the mother, his opponent and equal partner. Her love flows in endless streams of care and tenderness. She takes the father's efforts and adorns them with the beauty of affection, transforming their house into a home. She pours her very soul into ensuring that the tiny bud she holds in her arms blossoms into a radiant flower.

This game is unique, my friend. Whoever wins, both celebrate. Even in their defeat, they find joy. The beauty of this game lies in its selflessness—an arena fueled entirely by love.

Unlike other contests, where winners are filled with pride and losers with bitterness, this game leaves both players tearfully rejoicing in the shared triumph of their child. The mother and father may stand on opposing sides, but their hearts are united, playing a game of unconditional love.

It's the greatest match of all—a sacred bond, a priceless blessing bestowed upon every child. A game where one's victory brings joy to both players. Isn't it magnificent, my friend?"

As I concluded, I saw my friend lost in thought, his eyes reflecting newfound understanding. In this world filled with competitions and rivalries, the pure, undefeated love of parents stands as an eternal testament to the power of selfless devotion.

The Eternal Tree of Love

In moments of need, in times of pain, or simply when joy overflows, the first name on everyone's lips is «*Mother*» She is the sanctuary, the constant source of comfort. This has been true for me as well, proven time and again in my life.

The first word I ever uttered was "Maa." From that moment, in countless instances, I've sought solace in calling her name. Just hearing her voice or seeing her presence would lift half the weight off my heart. Before a child is even born, the divine has already prepared a gift—the mother.

From the very first breath, Mother governs and nurtures life, silently yet profoundly. Her guidance is like an unwritten law—molding us without words, protecting us with every silent gesture. Those who recognize and respect this divine influence are truly blessed.

A child's first cry of hunger is directed toward *Mother*. In pain, in joy, in moments of achievement, or even in defeat, it is her name that comes to mind first. She is the embodiment of every emotion we wish to share.

Often, I sit alone, reminiscing about the many sweet moments I've shared with my mother. Her presence in my life has been nothing short of a miracle.

Whenever I faltered, her face would reveal subtle signs that guided me. Her joy was evident in the twinkle of her eyes, silently approving my actions. Conversely, her silent pain in those same eyes reminded me to correct my mistakes. Every tear of happiness she shed felt like a blessing for my achievements. Her smiles, her glances, her every gesture—all were a language of love and wisdom.

Her eyes directed my path. Her eyebrows framed my every step with encouragement. Her nose, slightly tilted upwards, seemed like a compass pointing me toward my destiny. Her words, always measured and meaningful, became my scriptures.

Her arms were the cradle that soothed me. The rhythm of her heartbeat was the lullaby that comforted me. Her tender hands, ever outstretched, had the power to resolve any issue with the warmth of her embrace.

Her womb was the sacred temple where my life began. Her legs were the pillars that carried the weight of my existence. Her footsteps were the call to action that guided me toward the right path. My past is shaped by her thoughts. My present is the beautiful temple built on the foundation of her sacrifices. My future is the lush garden of hopes she sowed for me.

There is no deity greater than Mother. There is no guru more profound than her. Every breath we take from birth to death is a gift from her. To cherish this gift is to live a blessed life.

She is the truest friend, the selfless well-wisher whose love knows no bounds. Those who share a bond of friendship with their mother will find their lives filled with peace and joy. The contentment gained from her presence is unparalleled and complete.

We all come into this world as reflections of our mothers. This truth must never be forgotten. Every atom of our being carries her essence, every spark of light within us shines with her soul. To honor and revere this divine presence is to make one's life meaningful. To neglect or distance oneself from this truth is to invite darkness and despair.

The love of a mother is a treasure that can never be measured, a blessing that transforms every life it touches. Let us embrace this truth, cherish her love, and walk the path of life with gratitude and reverence for the eternal tree of love—Mother.

The Discovered Path

"I don't believe in God. More than that, I feel anger and hatred toward God," my friend declared firmly.

I had no right to challenge his belief, but I didn't agree with it. I felt compelled to try and change his perspective, knowing it would be difficult, perhaps impossible. But I had to understand what led him to such a conclusion.

"Why so much hatred? What wrong did God do to you?" I asked.

"Every misfortune in my life is because of God. I was once a devout believer, visiting every temple, church, mosque, and shrine I could find, pleading for my wishes to be fulfilled. Not a single prayer was answered. If God existed, wouldn't He have heard me? My despair, frustration, and emptiness—all stem from my belief in God. That's why I harbor so much anger and hatred toward Him," he explained.

"Did you stop trying and only rely on prayers?" I asked.

"No, I kept trying while also praying. If people don't cooperate, that's not my fault, right?" he countered.

"Then how can it be God's fault?" I replied.

He didn't agree. For him, God was a miraculous, all-powerful entity. To address his disillusionment, he first needed to let go of this perception. But I realized that I lacked the ability to fully convince him; long debates hadn't changed his stance.

"There's only one person who can answer your questions and resolve your doubts," I said.

"Who? Tell me, and I'll go wherever it takes," he responded.

"That divine being isn't far away; they're right in your home. It's your mother."

He burst into laughter, mocking my suggestion. After laughing for a long time, he regained his composure.

"You don't know my mother," he began. "She's uneducated, ignorant of the outside world, and content to stay in the kitchen. She's a timid woman who wouldn't dare step beyond the street without someone guiding her. Can she solve my problems? Can she perform the miracles that even God couldn't?"

I calmly began to explain.

"She is your mother, my friend. Every mother is a fountain of wisdom. Didn't she give you a form, nurture your life, and breathe vitality into your lifeless aspirations? Think about it.

True sages never claim omniscience. Those who admit they know little are the wisest. And among all beings, there is no one more enlightened than a mother.

Go to her, seek her counsel. Bow your head at her feet and pray. She will do everything in her power—her love, her strength, her devotion will be entirely for you. Only a mother can give herself so selflessly for her child.

There is no teacher, god, or guide greater than a mother. Go. Seek her. I speak from my own experience.

The divine presence you seek, the God you can see and feel, the God who moves and acts—it's your mother. Go to her, and you'll find your path."

My words seemed to strike a chord. He nodded silently, perhaps out of respect or friendship, and walked away. I returned home, satisfied that I had done my part.

A few days later, earlier than I expected, my friend came to visit me again. This time, his face radiated happiness. His eyes sparkled with newfound energy, and he wore a serene, luminous smile.

With great enthusiasm, he began to speak.

"I did as you said. I went to my mother. For the first time, I truly saw her greatness. I realized how ignorant I had been, how much pride and arrogance I carried. I used to see her as nothing more than a simple housewife, dismissing her as unimportant. I'm ashamed of that now.

I discovered that my mother is a divine presence, a goddess in human form. I have come to deeply respect her. My faith in God has been restored because I see God in her. There is no temple holier than her feet. I realised the fact that she is the treasure of love and empathy.

She filled me with a new spirit and renewed strength. Now, I feel ready to face any challenge. I've decided to tackle my problems head-on. I will fight tirelessly and stand tall, armed with the wisdom my mother shared with me.

Thank you, my friend, for showing me this path. Today, I understand who I am and what a mother truly is. I am proud, grateful, and above all, blessed."

His transformation was nothing short of miraculous, a testament to the power of a mother's love and wisdom.

—·—·—●—·—·—

The Joy of Discovery

Caught in the illusion that joy resides in wealth, I wandered aimlessly for years. I amassed more riches than I could imagine, and for a while, it felt fulfilling. But gradually, a profound truth revealed itself to me: wealth can bring comfort, but it cannot bring true joy. Determined to find joy, I set out on a quest, resolved to capture and bind it within my heart.

But every time I thought I had found it, it slipped away. Whenever I reached out, it evaded my grasp, leaving me longing.

I sought joy in the moonlight, basking in its serene glow, imagining that I could immerse myself in its beauty. But as I gazed, the clouds shrouded the moon, and the once-full orb waned into obscurity.

I felt it in the caress of a gentle breeze that touched my skin and thrilled my senses. I walked through nature, reveling in the embrace of the wind. But soon, the breeze stilled, turning stifling, and later, it rose as a tempest that instilled fear before vanishing.

I glimpsed joy in the vibrant blossoms, swaying gracefully and spreading their fragrance. Their aroma captivated me, and I sought solace in their presence. But soon, the flowers wilted, their petals scattered to the ground, taking their essence with them.

I heard joy in the babble of a flowing brook, calling out to me with its cheerful song. Drawn to its melody, I sat by its bank, entranced by the rippling waves that danced at my feet. Yet, the rushing waters could not offer permanence; their transient dance only left me wanting.

"Where are you, Joy? Are you hidden in the fleeting lightning bolts or the glimmer of distant stars? Do you reside in the warmth of the sun that fades into the chill of night? Are you in the gentle drizzle that turns into torrents, creating rivers that sweep everything in their path? Or in the majestic ocean waves that beckon, only to reveal their ferocity as I approach?"

I searched for joy in the songs of cuckoos, the dances of peacocks, the elegance of swans, and the playful chirping of parrots. "Are you in the bounding of hares, the sprint of calves, the grace of the lion, or the grandeur of the elephant?" I wondered.

I looked for it in the sweat of laborers, in the restful slumber of the weary, in the innocent laughter of children, and in the serene smiles of the aged. "Are you in the tender caress of a lover or hidden within my own restless heart?" I asked.

Joy appeared briefly, teasing me with its allure, only to vanish again. Exhausted and defeated, I returned home after years of futile searching, feeling utterly conquered by this elusive foe.

As I stepped into my home, I saw before me the very embodiment of all I had sought.

There stood my mother.

Her face radiated the glow of a full moon; her eyes shimmered like moonlit ripples. Her words were as fragrant as a garden in bloom, and her smile sparkled like a constellation. Her presence sanctified the space like a gentle breeze, and her voice carried the soothing melody of a babbling brook.

In her, I saw the majesty of the lion and the grace of the swan, the fortitude of the mountain, and the endless expanse of the sky.

In that moment, it dawned on me: true joy resides with my mother. She is the source of boundless joy, an eternal treasure. The happiness she offers is unending, unyielding, and incorruptible.

I understood then that the everlasting abode of joy is none other than a mother. Her presence is the sanctuary where joy is found. In her company, I found the joy I had spent a lifetime chasing. I realised that the joy surrenders itself to me, if i live like a Mother - spreading the wings of Love. Content and fulfilled, I rested by her side, soaking in the bliss she emanated.

The Eternal Worship

I have visited numerous places of worship across different faiths with friends on many occasions. While they seemed deeply moved and spiritually fulfilled, I often felt the rituals were superficial and contrived. Over time, I stopped visiting such places. Some experiences from those days, however, remain vivid in my memory.

Once, I accompanied a group of friends to a temple. There, the idols were adorned with flowers, fruits, and various fragrant substances. The priests performed elaborate rituals, and my friends urged me to fold my hands in reverence before the deities. I refused. They warned me that I would incur divine wrath. I replied that I would rather not bow to lifeless, unmoving stones. Their reaction was hostile, and as I walked away, they shouted, "Fool! Never return here!" I left, smiling.

On another occasion, some friends insisted I join them at a prayer hall. People there were singing hymns, swaying with devotion, and shedding tears as they prayed fervently. They asked me to kneel and join their chants. I refused again, saying, "I will not kneel before lifeless wooden symbols." They warned me of eternal punishment in the afterlife. I laughed, and they branded me a sinner, banishing me from the premises.

On yet another occasion, I visited a vast prayer ground at someone's insistence. A large crowd was bowing repeatedly, offering their prayers in unison. They asked me to bow too. I questioned, "Why bow to emptiness? What is there to seek in a void?" They became enraged, ready to attack me for my irreverence. I barely escaped unscathed.

My friends repeatedly tried to convince me to embrace their beliefs, but I could neither align with their faith nor disrespect their convictions.

I couldn't find divinity in the idols, statues, or structures I saw. I couldn't trust that they could protect or guide us. After much reflection and introspection, I arrived at a personal truth.

(They said a creator had made us, that a deity cared for us, guarded us, and directed us toward salvation. Others spoke of divine beings who preserved the innocence in us, guided us with wisdom, and nurtured us with compassion. These beliefs were poetic and beautiful, but I found them hard to accept.)

For me, no deity could surpass the essence of a mother. Rather than honoring divine figures once a week or on special occasions, I believed that revering a mother every day, every moment, was the greatest form of worship.

"My mother is my creator. The 'Supreme Being' everyone believes in is my mother. She nurtured me, tended to my hunger, and raised me with love and care. The 'Vishnu' within my soul is my mother. She dispelled my ignorance, shattered my illusions, and liberated me from false ties—she is my salvation. She is the 'Shiva' who vanquished my fears, strengthened my resolve, and made me victorious in life's battles. The boundless compassion of 'Christ,' the pure, unconditional love attributed to 'Allah,' and the peace, patience, and empathy taught by 'Buddha'—all reside in my mother.

A mother may leave this world, but the essence of 'motherhood' is eternal, a divine light that never fades. In all of existence, there is no form, no philosophy greater than that of a mother.

Living in her breath, dancing to the rhythm of her heartbeat, cherishing her words, and finding solace in her shade, aligning our steps with hers—this is the true essence of eternal worship we owe to our mother."

Life's Lesson

One day, unexpectedly, I fell ill. No matter how much I tried to strengthen my resolve, my body started to falter. When my own remedies failed, I had no choice but to admit myself to a hospital. Even after four days, I wasn't better. The doctors couldn't figure out the reason and suggested that my stress and worry might be affecting my body.

But what worry could I possibly have? I couldn't find the answer within myself. How could someone else understand what even I didn't know? The only person who might uncover this mystery was my mother—the eternal source of wisdom and comfort in our home. I called her and waited for her arrival.

Mother came, not in distress, but with the calm demeanor of someone experienced in navigating life's challenges. She sat by my side with the confidence of a healer. "You're fine. Don't worry," she said.

It was a stark contrast to what the doctor had been saying: "We're not sure what's wrong," or, "Let's run some more tests." The doctor, puzzled, had been asking me questions I couldn't answer. Mother, however, radiated certainty.

I introduced my mother to the doctor. He seemed curious. "Is this your mother?" his look seemed to ask. And mother's calm gaze seemed to respond, "Yes, and I know what's best for my son."

"Doctor, I need some time alone with my son," she requested. Her tone left no room for argument. Reluctantly, the doctor left, slightly bemused.

Mother sat silently, observing me closely. She didn't speak for a long time. Her penetrating gaze studied my every move and expression. Her wisdom wasn't learned from books or classrooms—it came from life itself, from years of understanding human nature.

Her silence was unnerving, and I began pacing the room. Holding a small mirror, I kept glancing at my reflection, as if searching for something. Mother watched me intently, her face calm, yet knowing.

After about thirty minutes, I sat beside her. She smiled gently and said, "I understand what's troubling you." Her words surprised me.

"What is it?" I asked.

"Your problem isn't physical. It's emotional. Deep down, you're troubled by the thought of aging. Without realizing it, you're worrying about losing your youth, your charm, and the status you hold. The fear that your wealth, position, and relationships might slip away is taking root in your subconscious. That fear has grown into a massive tree, casting a shadow over your health," she explained.

Her insight left me astonished. "How did you know?" I asked.

"I've been observing you for thirty minutes," she replied. "You keep glancing at the mirror, scrutinizing your face as if it holds answers. Your expressions reveal unease. You're fidgeting with your thinning hair, trying to make it look fuller. You're forcing yourself to stand straighter than your body allows. And you're walking faster than usual, almost as if trying to outrun something. But deep down, you're struggling to admit this to anyone, fearing they might mock you."

Her words struck a chord. "It doesn't matter if the body suffers, my child. What matters is that the mind remains healthy. Your mind is fighting a battle against natural changes, and that resistance is the root of your pain. You're clinging to illusions instead of embracing reality. That's the real issue."

She paused, her voice gentle yet firm. "Every human gets caught in a web of illusions, unaware of how to break free. This entanglement causes immense suffering. You need to understand that nothing in this world truly belongs to you—not your possessions, not your loved ones, not even your body. Detach yourself from these illusions. Recognize the truth and align yourself with it. Only then will you find peace."

"Your mind has no age, my dear. Don't try to age it prematurely. While the body will naturally age, don't resist its journey. Let there be harmony between your body and mind."

Her wisdom pierced through the fog in my heart. She was right—I had unknowingly let these fears creep in and weigh me down. My deepest fear, the thought of being separated from her, had clouded my mind. Her words showed me the destructive power of fear and the importance of freeing myself from it.

Resting my head in her lap, I found solace in her presence. "Mother, your words have opened my eyes. The doors of my heart, closed by ignorance, are now wide open. I've realized the burden of attachments and the beauty of living freely. From this moment, I'll strive to live with that freedom."

She smiled, her love radiating. "If your purpose is to serve this world selflessly, you will remain forever young in spirit. Read about the lives of great souls who found peace through detachment. Let their stories inspire you. Fulfill your duty, and you'll never need a doctor again."

"Mother, if you hadn't come, the world might have labeled me insane, and I'd have believed it. You're a master of all wisdom, and you've shown me a new path. I'm forever grateful to you."

"I know, my child," she said tenderly. "Even if you are far away, your thoughts sustain me. But I also know that without me, you wouldn't survive. Every mother feels this way. A mother's only desire is her child's happiness. If children live selflessly for the well-being of others, every mother will rejoice in eternal bliss

—∙—∙—●—∙—∙—

The Message from the Dream

I had a dream—a beautiful, unforgettable dream. It was extraordinary, full of light and meaning, leaving a lasting impression on me.

In the dream, I saw a radiant sunrise, and I found myself walking, unaware of my destination or purpose. I wandered along paths adorned with blooming flowers, beside streams that whispered soothing melodies, and under trees that swayed as if waving at me. Nature's beauty surrounded me, and the gentle greetings of kind souls felt like warm embraces.

I continued my journey, neither stopping nor knowing why I was walking. It was as though an invisible force called me forward, arms outstretched in welcome. With steady, confident steps, I moved ahead, feeling as if someone was guiding me, patting my shoulder to encourage me.

Eventually, I reached a marvelous place. Misty veils slowly lifted to reveal a breathtaking realm, unlike anything I had seen before. It felt like a heavenly abode or a dreamland. I stepped into this mesmerizing world.

Before me stood an elevated platform with numerous grand seats arranged atop it. Seated on those thrones were dignitaries whose faces I did not recognize, yet their presence filled me with an inexplicable sense of familiarity and warmth. They beckoned me with love, inviting me to approach. I walked toward them, awe-struck and overwhelmed.

Who were they? What were they going to say? As if I were an eager candidate about to face an interview, I stood before them, waiting for their words. They began to speak, their tone a mix of questions and answers, mysterious yet enlightening.

"Seeds are the essence of a tree. Clouds are the essence of rain. Light is the essence of darkness, and darkness the essence of light. An egg to a bird, a bird to an egg. A child to a mother, and a mother to a child. These are origins, inseparable. Have you forgotten your origins, blinded by your ego?

You boast of your progress and achievements, claiming they are entirely your doing. Who planted the seeds for your success? Who guided you, held your hand as you walked?

The breath within you, the energy that animates your being, the soul that shines in your essence—who is their source? Floating in the air of arrogance, you overlook the truth. Have you become blind despite having eyes?

Return to your world. Learn to walk forward while remembering to look back. Your past is the melody that welcomes your future. Do not sink into the quicksand of ignorance and pride. Go back and declare the truth. Walk the path of truth. Only then will you be allowed to enter this realm. Our invitation was only to show you yourself. To truly belong here, you must awaken to humility and wisdom. Go now. Go back."

As their voices faded, so did the ethereal world. Who were they? Divine beings? My ancestors? Or was it my own soul, speaking to me in myriad forms?

I began my return journey along the same path I had come. Slowly, the events of the day replayed in my mind.

That morning, I had been honored at a grand felicitation. My peers celebrated my three decades of accomplishments, showering me with praise. They spoke highly of me, and I basked in their admiration.

But now, I remembered how, intoxicated by the praise, I had fallen into a trance of pride. I had forgotten my parents—their love, sacrifices, and toil. I had failed to acknowledge the hands that had raised and guided me. In my speech, I omitted all mention of them. Overwhelmed by vanity, I had claimed my achievements as solely my own. Like many, I had become ungrateful.

The wise figures in my dream had awakened me to my reality. Their words opened the closed doors of my heart. Suddenly, I sat up in bed, shaken yet enlightened.

Before me stood my mother.

"Did you have a dream, dear?" she asked gently.

"No, Mother," I replied. "I found the truth. I discovered my roots. I have awakened."

Two Stones, One Sculpture

One day, an unexpected and distressing incident occurred at our office, shaking everyone to their core. It was unprecedented, deeply troubling, and demanded a severe course of action. Unfortunately, the responsibility of responding to the situation fell on me, leaving me feeling burdened and conflicted.

A male employee had behaved inappropriately toward a female colleague, humiliating her and tarnishing her dignity. The incident outraged everyone, leaving no choice but to terminate his employment immediately. Issuing that order weighed heavily on me.

When I returned home, my mother immediately noticed my troubled state. After learning about the incident, she too felt deeply saddened.

"This is a tough test of your leadership, my dear. It must have been agonizing to make such a harsh decision," she said, consoling me.

About an hour later, she approached me again. "Don't misunderstand my involvement in your office matters," she began cautiously, "but I have a suggestion for you."

Curious, I asked, "What is it?"

"Invite him to our home for lunch tomorrow," she said.

Her words stunned me.

"Mother, this is an office matter! If I invite him home, people will think I condone his behavior. Our organization's reputation could be at stake! How will this help the woman who suffered? Why are you suggesting something that could put me under even more scrutiny? How can this bring me any peace?"

As always, my mother responded with a calm and knowing smile.

"You've never disregarded my advice before, have you? Do you doubt that your mother would ever do something to tarnish your reputation or cause you distress?"

"Are you hoping to reform him, Mother? He's like a beast!"

"Until yesterday, wasn't he a human being?" she countered.

I had no answer to her question. Silent and contemplative, I finally nodded in agreement.

The next day, I met him and extended the invitation. Puzzled and uncertain, he reluctantly accepted. Truth be told, even I didn't fully understand what my mother intended. At that moment, I was merely the messenger, not the authority figure.

When he arrived, my mother welcomed him with the same affection she showed me. She treated him with kindness and respect, as if he were her own son. For a moment, I wondered if she had truly become his mother too.

He arrived tense and guilt-ridden, visibly uncomfortable. My mother, however, immediately put him at ease, touching his hands warmly and encouraging him to sit. Her gentle questions and genuine concern soothed him, breaking down his defenses. She served him a hearty meal, offering not just food but her boundless love and acceptance.

Once he felt more at ease, my mother began speaking.

"My child, listen to me carefully. Every sin has a remedy, every crime a punishment. Mistakes, however, have corrections. What you did was a mistake, and it can still be set right. That power lies in your hands.

Every being carries both humanity and animalistic instincts. Only humans have the discernment to elevate the former and suppress the latter. You must kill the beast within and awaken your humanity.

Like fire, you hold great potential. Fire can illuminate and nurture, but it can also destroy. Whether your fire warms or burns depends on the choices you make.

A fleeting moment of rage can cause destruction. It doesn't just consume your peace; it also inflicts pain on others. Patience and composure are the only tools to douse such flames.

Your actions may seem unforgivable to others, leaving you with no chance to redeem yourself. This is why you face the consequences you do now. Your behavior stirred a storm in your colleague's life and created chaos around you. Have you realized the harm you've caused?

How would your wife feel if she learned about this? A woman who loves, trusts, and admires you deeply—how would she respond to such a betrayal? What message does this send to your children, who look up to you and follow in your footsteps?

The trust of the women you work with, and the faith their families place in you, is not something you have the right to violate. Do you understand the gravity of your actions now?"

Overwhelmed by emotion, he broke down in tears, consumed by remorse. He vowed to seek forgiveness from the woman he wronged immediately. Then, overcome with gratitude, he knelt before my mother, calling her the sculptor who transformed the stone of his heart into something beautiful.

Witnessing this, I realized how shortsighted my decision had been. It might have escalated the situation rather than resolved it. My mother taught me the true meaning of wielding authority—to use it wisely and compassionately. With just one conversation, she reformed two people: him and me.

As we left together, I placed a hand on his shoulder, silently grateful for the invaluable lesson my mother had imparted. If everyone could think and act like her, this world would indeed become a haven of goodness and grace.

The Radiant Star

"Mom, why do you always get deceived? Don't you know anything else?"

Hearing my innocent question, my mother laughed heartily.

"Each person finds joy in different things. Maybe I find joy in being deceived," she replied. But her answer didn't seem right to me.

"Mom, everyone depends on you, makes excuses, and takes something from you. This world is full of deception! Only those who take survive, not those who give like you."

"Giving is divine; taking by force is demonic. You tell me, which one should I choose, my dear?"

"No matter what you say, people like you don't fit in today's world. You want to be good, but others twist goodness to suit themselves."

"Being good is not a mistake, my child. It gives life a sense of fulfillment, a joy beyond words."

"But mom, our life is for ourselves. The air we breathe, the money we earn—everything is for us, isn't it?"

"Try living for others just once. Experience the happiness of giving, of loving selflessly, and you'll want to do it again and again. Love, share, and you'll become like Shiva."

"Shiva? But he's a god! Can a human become a god so easily?"

"Shiva is not just a god, my child. Shiva means someone who does good for others. Isn't that what makes someone divine? A god cannot do evil, right?"

"I think it's best for a person to just live as a human. Becoming divine means losing everything, gaining nothing. Besides, no one remembers kindness these days. The world is full of ungrateful people. Maybe you don't know this because you don't see much beyond home. If you step outside, you'll realize how cruel people can be. Your philosophy doesn't work with the ungrateful. Today's rule is 'an eye for an eye.'"

Mom remained silent. Seconds passed. She kept looking at me with a gentle, unwavering smile on her face. She didn't even blink. My eyes, however, began to shift restlessly.

What was I doing? Was I debating with my own mother? Was this proof of my wisdom or my ignorance? Was I speaking from knowledge, or was I trying to understand something beyond my grasp?

More time passed. Mom's form felt vast, while I felt smaller. She seemed like a mountain, and I, a mere pebble. She shone like a star, like a divine flame lighting my inner wisdom. I felt like a lamp wick, ready to be ignited. Mom was transforming into a spiritual teacher, and I, a humble student. She was ready to teach, and I was finally ready to listen.

"The world isn't out there, my dear. It exists within us. We are our own world. Within us are the fiercest winds, the brightest flames, and the wildest storms. And beyond all that, we have the supreme power to control them.

Goodness and evil exist within us. Pain and joy exist within us. Suffering and happiness are our own creations. Hatred and greed take root inside us, but so does love. We are the gods; we are the demons.

You are used to seeing nature with physical eyes. But accept nature as your teacher, and new lights will shine within you. Become a great person who reaches out to help others.

Be like the sun, giving light to the world. Be like the moon, turning love into gentle moonlight. Be like the earth, providing shelter to others. Be like a great tree, bearing sweet fruits even when hit by stones. Be like a river, quenching the thirst of the needy. Be like a flower, spreading fragrance to all.

And when you do good without expecting anything in return, you will truly understand what goodness means."

Her words awakened something deep inside me. From that moment on, I stopped seeing the world as a cruel place. Instead, I worked on fixing the world within me. I learned to live joyfully, just like my mother.

The Melodious joy

When I started my new job, the organization arranged personality development classes for all employees. On the final day, a renowned personality development expert was invited as the chief guest. Everyone expected the event to be a grand success, with a large audience in attendance. To make it even more special, families were invited to participate.

At that time, my mother was staying with me. I decided to take her along. When I told her about the event, she agreed with enthusiasm.

On the day of the event, I attended with my mother. A huge crowd had gathered. The guest speaker, a highly acclaimed psychologist, was known for his ability to inspire and uplift his audience. His speeches were reputed to dissolve fears and dispel despair.

As expected, his lecture was mesmerizing. Every word resonated with wisdom, and the audience sat spellbound, hanging on to his every sentence. The hall was steeped in silence so profound that even a deep breath seemed loud. He cited quotes from great minds, delivering a profound speech with immense gravitas. Time seemed to fly as we listened intently.

Suddenly, my mother cleared her throat and gently tapped my hand. "Let's leave, my dear," she said.

Surprised, I looked at her. She seemed disinterested and restless, shifting in her seat.

"Mother, this is a valuable session," I whispered. "They've spent a significant amount to bring him here for us."

"I've heard all this before, my dear. These are the same teachings our grandparents and elders shared with us. Let's go," she replied.

"Mother, don't talk like a child. People might overhear. Sit quietly," I urged, trying to calm her. But she was insistent, like a stubborn child. Despite the awkward glances from others, I had no choice but to take her outside.

We left the hall and walked in silence for a while. Then we came across a park where children were playing. To my surprise, my mother ran toward them, joining their games and laughing with joy. She seemed to transform into a child herself, immersing herself in their world.

Her behavior unsettled me. Embarrassed, I rushed to pull her away from the children. She laughed as I dragged her to a nearby bench. Patting the seat beside her, she gestured for me to sit.

"Mother, we made a mistake. We missed the opportunity to learn profound wisdom. The man giving that speech is no ordinary person. People eagerly wait for his words. How could you leave that and choose to play with these children?"

"Playing with children brings immense joy, my dear. Isn't joy the ultimate purpose of knowledge, after all? Tell me, what knowledge do animals, birds, or insects need to live joyfully?"

"Mother, his words aren't ordinary. People pay to hear him speak. It's wisdom worth learning."

"My dear,

His words were not his own, my dear. He was simply repeating what he had read or heard, presenting it to us as if it were new. Moreover, I sensed arrogance in him, a belief that he knows everything and we know nothing.

True knowledge doesn't come from lectures, my dear. It comes from living and experiencing. It's not something to be heard and forgotten. It's something you internalize and practice.

It's foolish to think of someone else as great while you sit there passively. If you spend your time admiring others, you will lose sight of your own potential. Every individual possesses a unique quality. If nurtured, it can make them a pinnacle of excellence. If ignored, they remain an unshaped stone.

Never compare yourself to others, my dear. Compare yourself with who you were yesterday. Measure today against your past self. Shape yourself for the future. This is the essence of all wisdom and the root of true happiness.

Before books and personality development seminars existed, our ancestors lived by these truths and demonstrated them through their lives. Their footsteps are the true paths to joy. Embrace every moment with happiness. Savor every experience like animals, birds, and innocent children. Come, let's go home."

Her words revealed a new path to joy for me. By leaving the lecture, I found the opportunity to learn from my mother's wisdom. With a deep sense of contentment, I followed her home. I enjoyed a joyful of melody, in the company of my mother.

—·—·—●—·—·—

The Vast Ocean

"Schools teach us subjects, condense sciences into books, and make them accessible. But a mother's lap teaches us life itself. Through countless experiences, it shows us how to make life meaningful. While teachers are ready for us only when school opens, a mother is always prepared to teach us whenever we turn to her. I've learned far more in my mother's lap than in any school."

I often share these words with my friends and quietly repeat them to myself during solitary moments. It took me years to understand this truth, but once I grasped it, it became an unshakable belief. Although decades have passed since I left the halls of academia, my mother's lap remains my sanctuary.

My father was the one who fulfilled all my requests, and my mother was the one who met my every need. Leaving their protection to step into the outside world felt like stepping into an alien realm. It took me a long time to realize that not everyone would treat me with the unconditional love and care I received at home.

During my school days, I thought the world was an extension of my home, where my word was law, my desires were paramount, and my victories were celebrated by all. My arrogance grew. I wanted every victory to be mine and believed everyone else should bow to my success.

This mindset led to selfishness, intolerance, and an inability to accept failure. It turned me into my own enemy, creating conflicts with everyone around me. People began to see me as an uncooperative and troubled person.

Teachers at school called my parents and suggested that I see a counselor. My father, distressed, worried that I was becoming a lost cause. He spent sleepless nights thinking about me. Yet, amidst this storm of emotions, my mother stood calm and resolute, like a vast ocean. She convinced my teachers to grant me a break from school and stayed by my side without wavering.

She transformed the simplest moments into profound lessons. Watching a cuckoo sing, she'd explain, "It's singing a lullaby for its young." Seeing me enjoy catching fish in the pond, she'd gently say, "Let it go, son. It needs to go back to its mother."

She pointed to flocks of birds in the sky, swans in the lake, herds of cattle in green meadows, and children playing together without a care for differences. Through these, she taught me the beauty of coexistence.

She explained that no part of the body could function alone, no language could emerge from a single letter, and no symphony could arise from one note. The world thrives on interdependence. She showed me that even the tallest mountains rejoice when someone stands atop them and that true happiness comes from celebrating others' successes.

Slowly, the clouds of confusion lifted, and a new clarity dawned within me. My life began to sprout fresh shoots, and I felt as if my heart had grown wings. A world I had never seen before unfolded before my eyes.

One day, my mother took me to the edge of an endless ocean. She asked me to close my eyes and meditate. After a while, she asked, "Do you hear anything?"

"All I hear is the roar of the ocean," I replied.

"That's not a roar," she said. "The ocean is speaking to you. Listen carefully."

I tried again, and this time, I understood:

"I bear the weight of the earth. My calmness is the foundation of your peaceful life. If I rage, your very existence is at risk. For ages, I have weathered countless storms and remained tranquil. Within me lie treasures of pearls and jewels, and the wondrous worlds of countless living beings. I create the clouds that bring you water, and the waves that purify your air. Many sages and saints draw inspiration from me. I converse with the sun's brilliance and play with the moon's light. Even in the face of great calamities, I endure. Despite all this, I harbor no pride. I remain in my place, serene and content. Observe me, my friend. Be like me, and the infinite joy of existence will be yours."

The ocean's "roar" transformed into a gentle, profound language. I opened my eyes to find my mother smiling at me, her gaze as vast and nurturing as the ocean itself.

At that moment, I understood a profound truth. My mother, unlike any school, had learned life's values from nature. Her unwavering strength, boundless joy, and limitless love embodied the essence of life's lessons.

From that day, I accepted her as my guru. Gradually, I began to change, striving to emulate her. Today, the person I have become is a result of those changes. Whenever I face turmoil, I seek solace in her wisdom. For she is a divine ocean, holding treasures within, ready to share them with those who come to her shores.

—·—·—●—·—·—

A Delightful Feast

From the beginning of my life, my mother has been my guiding light, shaping my path and illuminating every shadow I faced. She is the rare flame of wisdom, dispelling ignorance and teaching life's lessons through love and compassion. Her silent guidance is a profound teaching in itself, making her the ultimate teacher on this earth. By simply watching and following her, I learned the meaning of life and found clarity in every path I took.

When I started my first job, my mother stayed with me for a while. At that time, I was unmarried and working for a prestigious organization headed by an enormously wealthy man. One day, the news came that his family was hosting a grand wedding, and every employee was invited. The scale and prestige of the invitation made all of us ecstatic. None of us had ever witnessed such opulence before, and the thought of attending such a grand celebration filled us with excitement.

Seeing my enthusiasm, my mother smiled warmly but said little. Days passed in joyful anticipation. On the fifth day, our housemaid arrived with an invitation card in hand. She had come to invite us—both my mother and me—to her daughter's wedding. She insisted we attend and even requested that we stay and help oversee the proceedings.

When I opened the card, I realized that her daughter's wedding was on the same day as my boss's grand celebration. Unsure of how to respond, I impulsively assured her that we would come and sent her on her way. Afterward, my mother asked me, "What do you plan to do?"

"We can't refuse the boss's invitation, can we? Besides, how can we attend a maid's daughter's wedding? We'll send her a small gift and make her happy," I replied.

My mother simply said, "Alright."

The day of the weddings finally arrived. After carefully instructing my mother about the house chores, I dressed up and left for my boss's mansion. The wedding venue was beyond description, radiating opulence and grandeur. The decorations dazzled, the lighting sparkled, and the entire setting resembled a celestial paradise. Beautifully dressed women greeted the guests, and young men attended to everyone with charm and politeness. Everywhere, there was magnificence.

My colleagues and I felt as though we were in a dream. For a fleeting moment, I wished I had brought my mother along to experience such splendor. Each corner of the venue displayed unrestrained extravagance, with prominent personalities from across the city gracing the event. Security measures kept guests from venturing too close to the central stage, ensuring exclusivity.

Later, a lavish banquet was served. It was an unparalleled feast, filled with such variety and richness that even tasting everything seemed impossible. Our stomachs full, we left the venue, marveling at the experience. Yet, amidst all this grandeur, one of my colleagues surprised us with his discontent.

"I didn't enjoy it at all," he said. "I wish I hadn't come."

His words shocked us, and we listened as he explained:

"This wedding had no love, no warmth, and no genuine connection. People were here, but their hearts were absent. Even the smiles and greetings felt artificial. Enemies embraced like friends, and friends burned with jealousy. It was all a facade—empty pomp and show. Relationships were nowhere to be seen; only money ruled this event."

No one could refute his observations. In silence, we left the venue, each lost in thought. His words rang true for me as well. Though the event was held at my boss's home, it felt as though we were strangers among strangers.

Returning home, I was surprised to find the house locked. My mother was nowhere to be seen. Suddenly, I remembered the maid's invitation. Suspecting my mother had gone to the other wedding, I rushed to the location.

As I neared the small house, I saw a simple canopy decorated with fresh flowers. Inside, about fifty people were seated, their faces glowing with genuine happiness. Everyone was warmly chatting, sharing stories, and connecting with each other. The bride's mother, dressed in a new saree, moved about, ensuring her guests were comfortable. Her husband invited everyone to eat, personally serving them with care. The bride, shy and radiant, sat beside her groom, smiling softly at his whispered words.

The bride's father saw me. He approached me with heartful affection. His eyes became wet with emotion and joy. He almost ran towards me and invited me forward. He started walking behind me humbly.

Amidst this scene of joy and intimacy, I spotted my mother. She sat on a beautifully adorned chair, surrounded by the bride's family. Her face glowed with contentment, her presence like a jasmine flower in full bloom. As I approached, she looked at me and smiled, her gaze filled with love and understanding. In that moment, I realized the true essence of celebration. It wasn't in grand decorations, expensive feasts, or illustrious guests. It was in the genuine connections, the warmth of human hearts, and the simplicity of shared joy.

Walking toward my mother, I felt an overwhelming gratitude for her wisdom. She had chosen love and authenticity over opulence, and in doing so, she had reminded me of what truly matters. I stepped forward, eager to embrace the lesson she had so silently taught me.

The Dance of Joy

It was an incident from years ago. Seeking tranquility, I wandered into the flower garden behind my house. As soon as I entered, the flowers seemed to welcome me with their enchanting fragrances. Breathing deeply, I began to stroll among them.

The flowers appeared to be in a state of divine bliss, their delicate stalks swaying gently as though nodding in greeting or rocking on swings.

"What's the occasion? Why are you all so joyous and ecstatic?" I asked, gently caressing the flowers with love.

"This is our daily ritual," they replied sweetly. "A while ago, our friends came to play with us and have now left. The joy they brought still lingers within us, resonating and filling us with ecstasy. This feeling will last until our play begins anew tomorrow morning. We are fortunate to have been born on this earth, and even more so, to bloom in this beautiful garden."

"Who are these friends of yours? The bees, perhaps?"

"No, the bees are not our friends. They come to steal the nectar we hold. Our true friends are those who fill us with life, not those who take it away."

"Who are these rare friends? May I know them?"

"They are indeed extraordinary friends, unmatched and unparalleled. Every twig, branch, tree, and even the soil here considers them companions. If you wish to know, ask the birds singing their melodies from nests hidden among the branches," the flowers suggested.

Intrigued, I moved forward. Looking up, I saw birds peeking out of their nests, craning their necks to look below.

Amidst the trees, the nests formed a bustling avian kingdom. Their melodious tunes greeted me, soft and sweet, inviting me with their cheerful calls.

"The flowers sent me to you. Can you tell me who your friends are?" I asked, hoping for an answer.

They chirped joyfully, responding with enthusiasm:

"Yes, they are our friends! One provides us water, another scatters seeds. They hold our nests in their hands, chat with us, and let us rest on their shoulders. We play with them, and they care for us deeply. They are protectors, nurturers, and lovers of all creation. If you want to know more, ask the cattle grazing with their calves in the meadow ahead."

With growing curiosity, I proceeded to the green pastures where herds of cattle grazed peacefully. As I approached, they surrounded me, their eyes filled with affection and curiosity.

"Who are your friends?" I asked them.

"They are divine beings sent by heaven for us," said one cow. "They play with us daily. One plays the flute, while the other showers us with love. They rest their heads on ours and speak to us with tenderness. If we are distressed, they are troubled. They stand as pillars of support, selfless and compassionate."

The love-filled descriptions of these divine beings stirred my thoughts deeply. I sat by a stream, contemplating who they might be.

The stream began to speak, its rippling sounds like a gentle melody. The sound reminded me of my mother's laughter, while its steady flow mirrored my father's unwavering energy. The shimmering sunlight on the water sparkled like my mother's radiant eyes, and the stream's ceaseless movement reflected my father's tireless dedication.

Suddenly, the realization dawned upon me. The divine beings that everyone revered were none other than my mother and father. They are the epitome of selflessness, giving without expectation and nurturing without pause. Their love is the invisible force that binds and uplifts all.

With this newfound understanding, I returned home, eager to see them. As I stepped inside, I froze in awe at the sight before me.

My parents appeared as a divine couple, engaged in a celestial dance of joy. Their movements were harmonious, embodying the eternal rhythm of creation. My mother's braid swirled like a garland, encircling my father's neck, while his breath seemed to dissolve the sweat on her brow. Her gaze pierced his heart with its intensity, and his laughter enveloped her like a cascade of blossoms. Their synchronized steps symbolized the unity of their journey, reflecting the cosmic dance of nature and life.

Witnessing their dance, I was overwhelmed with a profound understanding. The essence of life lies in giving, loving, and being loved. The beauty of two souls becoming one creates a masterpiece of harmony and joy.

To love and serve selflessly, as my parents did, is the ultimate truth of existence. Nature itself embraces such beings, celebrating their presence. Every atom of the universe reveres them, for they embody the timeless beauty and love that sustains all.

—·—·—●—·—·—

The Exquisite Eyes

In nature, there is day and night. We believe that day brings light, and night fills the world with darkness. It is human nature to despise the darkness and long for the light. However, the wisdom of great souls tells us that both are essential for the sustenance of creation.

In human life too, there are days and nights. We think of the day as a time for joy and experiences and the night as a bearer of sorrow and ignorance. While people embrace the vitality of the day, they tend to view the night as a time of inertia and unconsciousness.

But the truth is, we are the creators of the light and darkness in our lives. Our actions bring light into our world, or they cast shadows. To guide creation, the universe needs both the sun and the moon. Similarly, in our lives, the guiding sun and moon reside within our mother—a profound truth often forgotten by many. Ignorant of this, people trample the lamp at their feet and wander in the dark, searching for light elsewhere.

"Mother, your eyes are so beautiful. Perhaps that's why you can dispel the darkness of ignorance and light the flame of wisdom in everyone's life."

These words were spoken by a blind man. How could someone who had never seen the world describe the beauty of my mother's eyes? I couldn't understand how he grasped a truth that we, who can see, fail to recognize. Driven by curiosity, I spent days observing my mother's eyes with unwavering attention.

I noticed the flowers blossomed radiantly under her gaze, their petals glowing with new smiles. They nodded playfully as if conversing with her. A fresh fragrance seemed to emanate from them. As long as she looked at them, they radiated a timeless youth, as if they were gifted with eternal vitality. Even fallen flowers seemed to gather, laying themselves at her feet like a garland.

When my mother's eyes lifted toward the trees, a cuckoo hidden among the branches began to sing. Her gaze seemed to become the melody for the cuckoo's song, making it even more enchanting. Strangely, as soon as her gaze shifted, the song would stop, only to resume when she looked again. This divine interaction was a feast for my eyes, a mesmerizing play of beauty.

When my mother turned her head, a calf that had strayed from its mother suddenly bounded joyfully toward her lap, frolicking playfully. The mother cow approached, lifting her head to greet my mother. Stroking the cow's neck, my mother glowed with joy. The calf, delighted, wagged its tail between two mothers who seemed to share a sacred bond.

Watching my mother, who spread joy to everything around her while radiating serenity herself, left me overwhelmed with an indescribable feeling. It made me realize that even though I had grown up looking at her all my life, I had only truly seen half of her.

Determined to understand the blind man's words, I sought him out. I asked him, "How could you perceive the beauty of my mother's eyes when even we who can see fail to do so?"

"I saw it with the eyes of my heart," he said.

"How is that possible?" I asked in wonder.

"Your physical eyes see only what is visible. Those images affect your mind and guide your words and actions. Words, in turn, release unseen vibrations. When these vibrations are good, they inspire kindness and positivity; when bad, they bring harm. You believe that your mouth speaks, but there are countless unspoken words conveyed through the eyes and actions. These truths are visible to the blind and to animals, but, sadly, are often missed by those who can see."

"Your mother's words are filled with peace, kindness, compassion, love, and empathy. Her eyes reflect these virtues, a divine gift that all mothers possess. If we look with devotion, if we truly seek, she will share this gift with us too. That's what I did—I became like a child before her. That's why the divine granted me the vision to see her beauty. Don't live like the blind who can see; live like the mindful who act with love."

I listened to his words intently and gained a profound understanding. Bowing to this wise soul, who saw with the eyes of the heart, I returned to my mother, ready to see the world anew through the wisdom she embodied.

Ayodhya
(Impregnable)

Throughout my life, I achieved numerous victories. I stood tall without opposition, reaching a place where no one dared to challenge me. People began addressing me as "The Victor," and I shaped myself to deserve that title. Small mistakes I made during my childhood were quickly corrected, leaving no room for errors later in life. I became a victor without evoking envy, earning love and admiration from everyone who celebrated my triumphs.

Reaching these towering heights was no accident. The foundation was laid during my childhood. I was driven by an insatiable desire to win against everyone. Defeat was intolerable; satisfaction only came when I surpassed others. This innate competitiveness eventually sprouted into pride, which gradually evolved into arrogance. I began believing there was no one left to oppose me, confidently proclaiming my supremacy.

One day, while sitting alone, a strange thought crept into my mind. Having defeated everyone, I wondered if there was anyone left to conquer. Who else should bow before me and accept their defeat? This thought consumed me, and after much contemplation, a peculiar desire took hold of me—it was unlike any other I had ever felt.

I decided that my ultimate conquest would be defeating my mother. If I could triumph over her, I would become an eternal victor. But how? In what way could I compete with her?

I pondered this question for a long time but found no answer. Sitting by the riverbank, I gazed at my reflection in the still water. The clear, unmoving water reflected my face like a mirror.

Yet, my face did not appear calm. It was filled with unease, distorted by the turmoil in my mind. My reflection questioned me, looking back with an unsettling intensity.

"Would you really compete with your mother? Do you think you're greater than her? Are you trying to shatter a mountain with the strength of a fragile bubble? Do you truly believe that a few drops of honey are sweeter than an ocean of nectar? Having grown in your mother's lap, do you now seek to dance on her shoulders?

"Your thoughts are misguided. Your arrogance blinds you. Your ambitions, born of vanity, will lead to your downfall, much like the tyrants of history."

For a long while, I remained silent. Slowly, a sense of peace began to settle within me. Turning away from the water, I looked inward. My mother's radiant presence emerged in my mind, shining divinely. Her vast virtues unfolded before me, like a cosmic revelation. They dissolved the dark veil clouding my heart, guiding me toward enlightenment.

My mother appeared as a serene ocean, her waves of compassion washing over my restless soul. Her gaze, like soothing moonlight, enveloped me in tranquility. Her flowing hair resembled the dispersing shadows of the night. Her breath, like the chants of ancient scriptures, whispered the secrets of life into my ears. Her gentle smile was like rays of light, illuminating and uplifting me. Her tender hands felt like the branches of a tree, ready to support and protect me. Her heart became my sanctuary, her embrace my refuge. Her feet, the foundation of my future, offered me reassurance. She stood before me, the embodiment of a divine conqueror.

In that moment, I realized my folly. I lowered my head in humility, bowing before her. I sought her forgiveness for my misguided thoughts and childish arrogance.

"Mother, I was proud of being a victor. I foolishly thought I could conquer you, that I was capable of defeating even you. Forgive me for my immature thoughts, dear mother!"

My mother smiled. As always, her smile was filled with love, compassion, and kindness. Her golden words awakened my dormant soul.

"Desiring victory is not wrong, my child. But the one you must conquer is not others—it is yourself. Only when you overcome your inner flaws and weaknesses will you truly become a victor. Wanting to conquer the world is an unreasonable desire, my child. Defeat anger with peace, chaos with patience, desires with sacrifice, and arrogance with humility. Conquer evil with goodness. Refine yourself, and you will flourish."

Her blessings breathed new life into me. Inspired by her wisdom, I declared a war—not against others, but against my inner self. My journey toward self-perfection had begun.

The Fruit of Navarasas (Emotions)

A madman came to our village once. Nobody knew his name, where he was from, or why he had come. His odd behavior and peculiar attire made him a mystery to everyone. He took shelter under a tree, and if anyone approached him, he would shoo them away. If someone offered him food, he would throw it aside.

He never spoke to anyone. If he did, his words were sharp and unsettling, enough to make people uncomfortable. Children mocked him, and adults eventually stopped paying attention to him. They assumed he would leave as mysteriously as he had come.

At night, he slept with two stray puppies curled up beside him. Each morning, he would bathe in the nearby pond, wear the same tattered clothes, and return to his tree as though presenting himself for an audience.

If birds chirped on the branches above, he would respond in kind, mimicking their calls. He would draw letters in the air and then pretend to read them. When given good clothes, he would tear them and wear the scraps. If offered food in hand, he would reject it; if served, he would eat.

When asked, "Madman, where are you from?" he would reply, "I come from a good village. This is the crazy village, and all of you are mad!" He would then laugh at his own response.

Though children teased him, he would affectionately chat with them. One day, as we all sat around him, he started asking us strange, thought-provoking questions. None of us could answer him. His words left us puzzled and embarrassed.

One statement he made, however, left a deep impression on me:

"Everyone in this village is mad. You chase after things you don't have, without knowing what you're looking for. You swing from branch to branch, leaving one behind while grabbing another, never setting foot on solid ground. You are blossoms that have yet to bear fruit. You must bloom fully and transform into fruits that offer sweetness to the world. But not ordinary fruits—become the fruits of *Navarasas* (nine emotions). Go, read not books but the pages of life. Go and transform yourselves."

Waving his stick dramatically, he drove us away.

Back home, his words echoed in my mind. Was he truly mad? Or was there a deeper meaning to his strange behavior? His statement about "Navarasa fruits" intrigued me. Were there really fruits that embodied the nine emotions? The idea seemed impossible but also profound.

I shared his words with my friends, but they had already forgotten him. I asked my father, who laughed it off, saying, "Madmen's words have no meaning." I sought the advice of learned teachers, but they dismissed it as nonsense. Finally, I turned to my mother. She was my refuge, the one who always had answers. I recounted the madman's words to her, seeking clarity.

My mother fell silent, her expression thoughtful. After a long pause, she opened her eyes and smiled gently.

"The man you call mad is no madman, my son. He is a great soul, a realized being who has renounced everything. The 'Navarasa fruit' he spoke of is real, but it is not tangible. It is a rare fruit, visible only to those who close their eyes to the material world and open their inner vision. This fruit is none other than the human mind itself.

"A person's behavior is the outcome of the *Navarasas*, the nine emotions. To live as a complete human being, one must embody all these emotions in harmony:

1. Love (*Shringara*) – Show unconditional love to all living beings.

2. Laughter (*Hasya*) – Speak words that bring joy and do not hurt others.

3. Wonder (*Adbhuta*) – Achieve things that inspire awe in others.

4. Courage (*Veera*) – Overcome cowardice and face challenges bravely.

5. Peace (*Shanta*) – Confront adversity with calm and patience.

6. Compassion (*Karuna*) – Be empathetic and kind toward others.

7. Anger (*Raudra*) – Channel righteous anger to confront and suppress inner flaws.

8. Fear (*Bhayanaka*) – Recognize and combat deceit, hatred, and dishonesty.

9. Disgust (*Bibhatsa*) – Use this emotion to distance yourself from immoral actions.

"When a person masters these emotions, they become a complete human being. The madman's words were not mere ramblings; they were a profound teaching. He asked you to grow into individuals who embody these nine emotions. If everyone in the world became like this, the world would shine with the light of wisdom."

Her explanation illuminated the truth for me. The madman's words were not madness but profound wisdom. Bowing to my mother, I resolved to cultivate the *Navarasa fruit* within myself and live as he had taught.

Beauty of Jubilation

One day, my friend and I were sitting in a park, enjoying a conversation. Suddenly, a caterpillar crawled onto his foot. The moment he noticed it, he shuddered in disgust and hastily brushed it off with a dry twig, flinging it far away. The poor creature lay motionless for a while before slowly crawling into the bushes, disappearing from sight.

I didn't like how harshly he treated the innocent creature. He explained that he found caterpillars repulsive, though he would have happily welcomed a butterfly and even played with it. Despite knowing that caterpillars transform into butterflies, his behavior perplexed me.

This wasn't the first time I'd witnessed such contradictions. As a child, I once played with a friend until his mother came along, pulled him away, and scolded him for playing risky games. My own mother, on the other hand, always encouraged me to play, often watching over me to ensure I was safe.

Why these conflicting attitudes? Why does one find beauty in something while another finds it unpleasant? Why is one person's good another's bad?

A poet might find inspiration in the murmurs of a flowing river, composing verses of beauty. Yet another might feel disturbed by the same sound and leave in frustration. An artist might be enchanted by a beautiful woman's visage, eager to immortalize her in his painting. But a recluse might sigh at her fleeting beauty, indifferent to her charm.

A singer may draw melody from a cuckoo's song, losing himself in its harmony, while another person might throw stones at the bird, annoyed by its noise. One delights in the cold of winter, while another shivers and wraps up tightly. One toils under the blazing sun, unbothered by the heat, while another seeks refuge in the cool of an air-conditioned room.

Such differences puzzled me for a long time. Why doesn't the same beauty appeal to everyone? Where does joy truly reside? If beauty isn't in the object itself, where is it hidden?

Are the flaws in the object or in the observer's perception? Everyone's eyes see the same scene, their ears hear the same sound, their skin feels the same texture, their nose smells the same fragrance, and their tongue tastes the same flavor. Yet their reactions differ. Why is this so?

Does absolute beauty exist in this world? If it does, why doesn't everyone perceive it? Why is beauty subjective, and what defines it? Could it be an illusion?

These questions haunted me. I turned to my mother, the only person who could offer clarity. My mother, who never read the scriptures but embodied their essence, was my guiding light. I shared my confusion with her, seeking her wisdom.

Her face lit up with joy at my curiosity. I knew she would have the answer, and I eagerly listened as she began to speak.

"Our body functions according to the food we eat. The body, in turn, influences the mind. The state of our mind governs our senses. The eyes see an object, but it is the mind that interprets and reacts to it. The object itself doesn't evoke joy or sorrow—it is our mind's perception that creates these feelings.

The problem isn't with the outside world but within us. The external world is neutral; it is our internal turbulence that creates biases. That's why scriptures teach us to see beauty in everything. Joy isn't external—it resides in the pinnacle of every human being's mind. It is divine, eternal bliss. This is what sages call *Brahmananda*—the ultimate, everlasting joy. To experience it, one must prepare the body and mind through discipline and self-reflection.

Examine your life. Observe yourself. Rectify your shortcomings. When your mind achieves balance, you will move beyond fleeting pleasures and pursue eternal bliss. Let others' discontent not disturb your peace. Be a beacon of inspiration for those around you, my child."

Her words resonated deeply. They illuminated the path to finding true joy—not in fleeting objects or superficial pleasures, but in the eternal harmony within. The beauty of life, I realized, lies in preparing ourselves to perceive and share that joy with the world.

The Whimpering

Not long ago, I went on a family trip with my wife, children, and my mother. It was one of the most cherished moments of my life, filled with unforgettable memories from a week-long journey.

Surrounded by breathtaking natural beauty, we relished every moment, soaking in the serenity and joy of the picturesque landscapes. On the last evening, as we sat sipping coffee, reminiscing about the trip, I noticed something unusual. Everyone's face radiated happiness, but my mother's expression was different. She seemed troubled, lost in deep thought, her face shadowed by an unspoken sorrow.

Perhaps the thought of the trip coming to an end weighed on her, I wondered. Hoping to lighten her mood, I asked if we should extend the trip for a few more days, just for her. But instead of answering, she gave a faint smile and walked away. She went to the balcony, sat down, and gazed at the distant mountains.

I followed her and asked, "What's wrong, Mom? Why do you seem so troubled?"

"These past days may have brought joy to all of you, but for me, they've been heavy, like a burden," she said.

"I understand, Mom. Father's absence leaves a void that nothing can fill. This trip was my attempt to give you some solace, a small way to bring you happiness."

"That's not it, my child. These past days, while you were enthralled by nature's beauty, nature spoke to me. And it filled me with grief."

"Nature spoke to you? What did it say?" I asked, puzzled.

She began to speak, her voice heavy with emotion.

"The flocks of birds soaring in the sky spoke to me. They told me about how, for generations, they built their homes on sturdy tree branches, swinging joyfully and raising their young in warmth and safety. Storms came and went, but they thrived in the shelter of lush green trees. They lived believing this was their eternal haven. But now, humans have torn down their homes, cut down the trees, and left them scattered and homeless. 'We are leaving,' they said, 'fleeing to unknown lands, beyond the reach of humans who destroy everything in the name of progress.'

"The clouds that poured rain were not joyful, as you all imagined. They were shedding tears. They mourned how poets once praised their silvery beauty, but now they bear a pale, weary face, laden with sorrow.

"The rivers spoke of their pristine waters, now defiled by pollution. The trees, their broken branches and uprooted roots, lamented their destruction. Forests that once stood as proud guardians of life now sing mournful songs of despair.

"Even the protective layers of the earth, which shield us from the sun's fierce heat, are being pierced, leaving the earth mother scorched and weeping. What you see as beautiful landscapes today are but the remnants of a once-glorious creation now fighting for survival. The earth's anguish, the tears of every element—air, water, soil, and sky—permeate everything around us.

"The grandeur of this trip only reminds me of how much has been lost. Nature, once a harmonious symphony, now cries out in pain. Humans, who are meant to be part of this harmony, see themselves as rulers, exploiting and harming all other beings.

«Nature's collective voice is crying out: 'Of the 84 lakh species on earth, humans claim to be the most evolved, the most intelligent. Yet, no creature is more cruel than humans. The earth mother endures their atrocities in silent agony, every moment.' That cry reaches every living being except humans."

Mother fell silent, her words hanging heavily in the air. Her steady demeanor, always a source of strength, now revealed a deep vulnerability, a sign of the profound impact of humanity's actions on her heart. If someone as steadfast as her could feel such sorrow, it was a sign of the grave path humanity was treading.

Though Mother's reflections might seem poetic, they held undeniable truths. Humanity is digging the ground it stands on, cutting the branch it sits upon, and destroying the nest it builds. The beauty we see hides a deep pain.

Unable to console Mother or offer any meaningful words, I too sat in silent reflection, feeling the weight of the earth's lament.

—•—•—●—•—•—

Love That Blossomed

A young woman started pursuing me, claiming to be in love. For a long time, she followed me persistently. I tried to convince her that it was impossible, but she wouldn't listen. She confronted me directly, sent me love letters, and even sent messengers with her pleas. Her unyielding pursuit became a significant problem for me.

She begged me repeatedly, saying, "Marry me. I'll dedicate my heart and soul to you. I am ready to devote my life to you."

I explained, "I'm married and have children. You need to let go of this idea." But she didn't relent. "So many men have multiple wives. Haven't you read stories or seen real-life examples? I don't have any objections," she argued.

Ironically, one of my friends deeply admired her and loved her with all his heart. I explained this to her and tried to redirect her feelings toward him, but she ignored it entirely.

I was trapped, unsure of whom to confide in. I couldn't discuss this with my wife, nor with others, as it might tarnish her reputation. Feeling helpless and burdened, I spent days seeking a way out.

Fortunately, my mother came to visit us during this period. I confided in her and shared the entire situation. My mother, calm and wise as always, advised me to continue dissuading the young woman with love and patience. "Do not hurt her feelings or humiliate her, no matter what. Genuine love can't bear rejection easily, and any harshness could lead to unintended consequences," she said.

"This is a delicate issue, my son," she continued. "Handle it with both care and compassion."

Her advice seemed even more challenging than the problem itself. "Reject her without hurting her? How is that possible?" I thought. Yet, trusting my mother's wisdom, I approached the young woman, still grappling with uncertainty.

She ran to greet me with eyes full of hope, her heart brimming with love, and an unshakable confidence that I wouldn't turn her away.

I knew her love was pure, her heart untainted, and her intentions genuine. Her love was sincere devotion, not fleeting desire.

For almost an hour, I earnestly explained my commitment to my family and gently asked her to redirect her love to my friend, who admired her deeply. But she stood firm, refusing to yield.

Faced with her unwavering love, I realized my limitations. Unable to convince her, I said, "Convince my mother. If she agrees, I will think about it."

She leapt with joy, exclaiming, "I'll win her over in no time!" Determined, she set off to meet my mother.

My friend, meanwhile, had been devotedly in love with her for three years. He loved her with all his heart and was ready to sacrifice everything for her happiness. He came from a prosperous family and had turned down numerous other proposals, all for her. They seemed like a perfect pair created by destiny.

The young woman met my mother and poured her heart out, seeking her blessings and acceptance.

"Let's see," my mother said. "Visit us regularly for the next four days." The young woman agreed eagerly, her confidence bolstered by this partial victory.

By the end of the first day, she and my mother had become close friends. They began sharing their thoughts and engaging in deep conversations. It was as if they had opened their hearts to each other, creating a bond that grew stronger with every passing day.

Initially, it seemed like the young woman was dominating the conversations. But soon, I noticed her melting before my mother's wisdom and presence. Over time, she transformed. Her youthful innocence evolved into maturity, and her laughter became genuine and radiant. Their friendship blossomed beautifully, filled with mutual respect and joy.

On the fifth day, the young woman asked to meet me at the park. When I arrived, she looked like a changed person, exuding an air of peace and clarity.

She spoke openly, "I spent time with your mother, listening to her and observing her. I saw a complete woman in her—one who embodies serenity, wisdom, unshakable joy, purity, and compassion.

"I began to see through her eyes. She helped me realize that the man I love is extraordinary, but so is the one who loves me. True love isn't about clinging but about understanding and choosing wisely.

"I have decided to embrace the love of the man who has been patiently and devotedly waiting for me. Please forgive me for causing you any trouble. Before he changes his mind, I must go to him and offer him my heart."

She started to leave, but my friend, who had been standing nearby, rushed toward her. He knelt before her, hands outstretched, as though pleading with the divine for a miracle. His sincerity moved everyone.

When I turned around, I saw my mother. I was surprised to see her there, but she stood with a gentle smile. My friend held the young woman's hand and led her to my mother. He bowed his head as my mother placed her hands on his, blessing the couple.

With a radiant smile, my mother looked at me. She gestured that it was time for us to leave. Leaving the couple to their newfound happiness, my mother and I quietly walked away.

—·—·—●—·—·—

The Fragrance of Love

One day, my mother expressed a strange wish. She wanted to visit the village where she was born and raised after nearly fifty years.

"Why now, Mother? Who do you think would still be there?" I asked.

"They say a place you're born is like your mother. I want to see how my village looks now," she said with a childlike excitement. "Maybe some of my childhood friends are still there. Will you take me there, my son?"

What greater joy could there be for a child than fulfilling their mother's wish? I immediately agreed. She lit up like a little girl, brimming with happiness.

One fine day, we set out for the village where my mother had spent her early years. Her eyes glistened with tears of joy as she roamed around, revisiting the places that had been her world.

The village had changed significantly. Every corner was filled with new faces. The house where my mother was born had been replaced by a new one. Familiar faces were nowhere to be seen.

Still, some things remained—her school, the fields where she once ran and played, the trees that had cradled her swings. She spent about two hours there, lost in a world of memories, connecting with every speck of the soil, every rustle of the trees. She was visibly overwhelmed, her joy spilling out in smiles and tears.

By the afternoon, we reached the edge of the village, where an old, dilapidated hut stood.

"My childhood best friend used to live here. I wonder if she's still around or if she moved away," my mother said wistfully.

There was no sign of life around the hut. But for her sake, I decided to take a look. Inside, it was surprisingly tidy, with neatly drawn rangoli patterns and well-arranged things. In one corner, an elderly woman was sitting and reading a book. She seemed about the same age as my mother. I felt a spark of hope that this could be her friend and called my mother inside.

They looked at each other for a few moments, searching for recognition. Then, as though time had never passed, they embraced each other, tears flowing freely. Words were unnecessary as their hearts spoke volumes. Their faces lit up with a joy that only reunited souls can feel.

Gradually, they began sharing their stories, diving into an ocean of memories. I sat quietly, watching their heartfelt conversation unfold like a beautiful scene from a movie. Decades of stories flowed between them without pause.

Suddenly, her friend dashed outside and returned with two guavas she had plucked from her backyard. Without hesitation, they began feeding each other, taking bites from the same fruit. It was as if they were two children again, unburdened by the world. Their shared joy and love transformed a simple act into something extraordinary.

Watching this, a childhood story I had read came to mind—the tale of a king who, exhausted from hunting, was offered food by a poor tribal woman. The woman, out of love and care, first tasted the food to ensure its quality before offering it to the king. The king, overwhelmed by her selfless love, ate with gratitude.

This was no story; it was happening before my eyes. These two friends were like royalty, sharing a love so pure that they seemed unaware of any differences. To them, love was all that mattered.

I recalled my childhood when my mother would offer me food she had first tasted herself. At the time, I felt uneasy and even worried that she was eating my share. One day, I complained to my father about it. He smiled and said:

"Your mother isn't taking your food, my son. Out of love, she's tasting it first to ensure it's perfect for you. If you don't believe me, try the food she leaves for you without tasting."

Following his advice, I tried it. The untouched food tasted bland, lacking the warmth and love I had always felt in her offerings. I ran back to my father and told him what I'd discovered.

He smiled again and said, "That's your mother's love, son. Her touch turns everything into nectar. True love knows no boundaries or reservations. It's selfless and pure. Look at the birds. They fly far and wide to fetch food, only to regurgitate it for their young ones. That's love, a divine phenomenon, not something created by man."

Since that day, I embraced my mother's love as a divine blessing. Every morsel she offered, every drop she shared, I accepted with reverence, savoring the sweetness of her love.

Now, watching my mother and her friend share guavas in the same spirit, I was reminded of the enduring beauty of love—a love that transcends time, age, and circumstances. In that moment, the sweetness of their bond was the purest form of joy.

—·—·—●—·—·—

Blindfolded Bliss

A beautiful memory from my childhood often fills my heart with joy—a playful, unforgettable game that remains etched in my soul. My mother, father, and I played together, and though it was a simple game, its charm and meaning made it extraordinary.

The game was simple: blindfold one person, and they had to find and catch another. The first round began with my mother blindfolded, and her goal was to catch my father. I was tasked with being the referee, a duty I proudly took on, feeling like a judge presiding over a delightful contest.

Father moved gracefully, staying just out of her reach, his steps light and playful. Mother, blindfolded but determined, reached out her hands, trying to sense his presence. It wasn't just a game—it was a dance, a silent exchange of affection between two hearts that transcended words. Their movements had a rhythm, a joy that lit up the moment.

Father's every step seemed like part of a well-rehearsed dance. He teased her, clapping or snapping his fingers nearby but moving away before she could catch him. Mother, meanwhile, followed the sounds, her hands extended as if she were carrying invisible garlands meant for him. Her smile, even behind the blindfold, glowed with delight.

And then, suddenly, Father stopped. He saw the beads of sweat glistening on Mother's face, saw her effort, her unwavering determination. Something softened in him. Gently, he stepped closer, allowing her to catch him. She removed the blindfold with a triumphant smile, but in her victory, there was no gloating—only love. Father had lost, but his loss was sweeter than any win because it brought joy to her.

Now it was Father's turn to be blindfolded. Mother moved like a flowing river, swift and elusive. She laughed and teased him, saying, "I'm here! Come catch me if you can!" She danced, her steps as graceful as a swan's glide, always just out of his reach. It was as if they were enacting a celestial dance, a divine duet of love.

Father, with the precision of a hunter, followed her sounds and movements, trying to close the gap. But Mother was quick, her laughter ringing like music, her movements light and playful. I watched in awe, mesmerized by the harmony and joy between them. Time seemed to stand still as they danced around each other, their love filling the air.

When the timer neared its end, Mother suddenly stopped running. She turned and embraced Father, resting her head on his chest. In that moment, she surrendered, and his arms encircled her with a protective warmth. She had chosen to let him win, and in doing so, both had won.

Now, it was my turn to be blindfolded. My parents tied the cloth around my eyes, their voices filled with encouragement.

"Remember, no cheating!" I warned, determined to play fairly and win. I was focused, every sense tuned to detect their movements. Mother dodged with skill, her laughter echoing as she evaded my grasp. I pushed myself harder, running, reaching, but she was always a step ahead.

The more I tried, the more elusive she became. Exhaustion began to creep in, but her laughter and presence spurred me on. Father, my referee, called out, "Don't give up! You can do it!"

I took a deep breath, centering myself. I thought of Mother—her scent, her warmth, the sound of her anklets, the rustle of her movements. Slowly, her presence became clearer to me, not through sight but through something deeper. I could feel her love guiding me.

Her soft whispers, the faint tinkle of her anklets, the gentle breeze of her movements—all led me to her. Finally, with a burst of energy, I reached out and caught her, wrapping my arms around her waist. I held her tightly, unwilling to let go.

Mother laughed, her joy lighting up the moment. Father clapped and praised me, his pride evident. In that embrace, I felt an indescribable happiness—a connection that transcended the game, a love that bound us all.

This simple game, filled with laughter and love, remains one of the most precious memories of my life. It wasn't just a game—it was a celebration of love, trust, and the unbreakable bond we shared. Even now, whenever I close my eyes, I can relive that day, the joy of those moments filling my heart anew.

—•—

The Wondrous Three

Among the many cherished moments that shaped my life, one stands out vividly. A memory so profound, I find myself reminiscing about it time and again.

One evening, tired from playing with friends, I returned home to find my parents engrossed in a conversation. Like two birds nestled in a warm corner of their sanctuary, they sat close, lost in each other's company.

My father had taken my mother's palm in his hand and was examining it intently. A gentle smile played on her lips as she watched him, her eyes filled with love and curiosity. My father began to read her palm, speaking with a surprising depth that captivated her.

"Father knows palmistry?" I wondered in amazement. This was something I had never noticed before. Did Mother know this? Or was she just playing along? Uncertain but intrigued, I quietly watched them. His words were soothing, filled with affection, and the scene unfolded like a poem written by life itself.

As he examined her palm, he shared insights about her life. My mother listened, enraptured. Her smile widened with each revelation, her face glowing with a childlike delight. He described her auspicious traits, painting her as a picture of beauty and virtue.

"Are there no flaws in me?" she teased.

"Why search for flaws when none exist? Even the thought of finding flaws in you is a flaw itself," he replied with a twinkle in his eye.

"Did you marry me because of these auspicious traits?" she asked.

"No. I married you because I fell in love with your heart. Your beautiful heart drew me in and made me yours. What about you? What did you see in me?"

"I saw your broad chest," she said with a mischievous smile. "It radiated courage and strength, and I knew it would be my safe haven."

Their conversation was tender, filled with gentle humor and unspoken love. I sat there, mesmerized, unable to take my eyes off them.

Father then shifted his focus to Mother's neck. Her neck stood tall and graceful, like a lotus blooming in serene waters. With the delicate touch of his fingertips, he gently caressed it, noticing something remarkable.

"Have you ever seen these three lines on your neck?" he asked. "They are rare, a mark of divine grace found in only the most blessed women. These lines signify beauty, prosperity, and goodness in abundance. People notice the ornaments you wear, but I see the unmatched elegance of these lines."

Mother burst into laughter, her joy resonating like temple bells and bubbling streams. Her laughter filled the room, enveloping me in its warmth.

My heart swelled with happiness. How fortunate was I to witness such a beautiful moment between them—a bond so pure, so full of love.

Noticing me watching, they beckoned me closer. Pulling me into their embrace, they shared their warmth and love.

"A blend of courage and beauty," I declared, "that's what made me."

I carried this memory with me, cherishing it as a guiding light. Those three lines on my mother's neck became symbolic to me, shaping my journey in ways I couldn't have imagined.

Where my father saw beauty and auspiciousness, I saw three paths—three guiding principles that led me through life.

- The topmost line became my *Sattva Guna*, inspiring wisdom, clarity, and a sense of purpose.

- The middle line was my *Rajo Guna*, fueling my drive, courage, and determination to succeed.

- The lowest line represented *Tamo Guna*, sparking my introspection, self-awareness, and a thirst for knowledge.

These lines reminded me to balance my actions, reflect on my past mistakes, and move forward with clarity and strength. They taught me to create a harmonious present while paving a golden path to the future.

To this day, those three lines remain etched in my memory—not just as marks of beauty, but as the sacred numerology of my life. They symbolize the essence of who I am and what I strive to become.

The Hidden Force

A shadow puppet show was organized near my house. A troupe had come from afar, setting up camp for a week and performing every night. Their performances, weaving together countless mythological tales, captivated everyone.

It was a breathtaking display of artistry and storytelling. The intricate movements of the puppets, accompanied by music and narration, left the audience spellbound. On the final night, the villagers honored the performers with heartfelt applause and tokens of appreciation.

Each night, I would return home enchanted but restless, replaying the mesmerizing scenes in my mind. Too young to grasp the technicalities, I wondered how the lifeless puppets danced so gracefully. It wasn't until the third night that I sneaked behind the screen to discover the secret: a group of skilled artists was manipulating the puppets, singing, and narrating from behind the scenes. The mystery unraveled, but my admiration for their craft remained intact.

I began to ponder: *Who deserves the credit—the puppets or the puppeteers?* Without the puppeteers, the puppets wouldn't move; without the puppets, the artistry wouldn't exist. Yet, I felt there must be a greater force, someone or something beyond both.

I shared my thoughts with Mother. She listened, smiled, and said, "The beauty of the puppets lies in the skill of those who control them. But neither can exist without the other. They are interdependent, completing each other."

Our discussion shifted from puppets to people.

"Who moves us, Mother?" I asked.

"Humans are like those puppets," she replied. "We, too, are moved by a hidden force—an invisible energy that resides within us."

"Who placed this energy in us?" I pressed.

"That's a profound question, my dear. Some believe it is an inherent part of our being. Others say it is a divine force, a gift from God, the Supreme Power. They believe this energy is the soul, a fragment of the Universal Soul that pervades everything. These are philosophical matters that only life experience can unravel for you. For now, enjoy the performance and ponder its beauty," she said, pacifying my restless mind.

I followed her advice and carried on with life. Yet, the question lingered, gnawing at the edges of my consciousness.

At times, I felt this energy within me was my sole guide. But where had it come from? If it originated from the universe, what was its source? Was it drawn in like breath, journeying with me until it departed one day? And where did it return? To some greater force? If so, what is the origin of this universal power? Is it God?

I wrestled with these questions for years. *Is God male or female? Where does God reside? What form does God take?* How could this unseen force guide countless lives, animate every being, and orchestrate such complexity?

For half my life, these doubts tethered me like chains, imprisoning my thoughts. Then, one day, a revelation struck me like lightning. It was as if a flame of wisdom ignited within me, dissolving my doubts and unraveling the web of questions. The truth unfolded before me.

The energy that fills my being, the force that moves me—it is Mother.

The universal energy, the source of my existence—it is Mother.

The soul within me—it is Mother.

The foundation of that soul, the Supreme Soul—it is Mother.

The Creator, whom I called God—it is Mother.

The breath that sustains me, the constant ebb and flow of life—it is Mother.

The soul, the Supreme Soul, the divine energy, the universal force—whether they have form or not, whether they are visible or invisible, all these merge into the essence of Mother.

I realized that I am but a puppet. The unseen force, both near and distant, visible and invisible, living its own life while animating mine—that force is Mother. All the light within me is but a reflection of her radiance.

———•———

The Graceful Refuge

During my childhood, an incident left a profound imprint on my heart—a small squabble with my father over how he affectionately teased my mother.

He often called her, "*Oh, slender-waisted one, come here!*" I found this phrase disrespectful and couldn't tolerate it, even though my mother took it with grace and humor. One day, when he repeated it, my childish anger exploded, and I leapt at him, grabbing him by the collar in protest.

To my surprise, he laughed heartily, his eyes twinkling with delight at my innocent defense of my mother's dignity. He shared the episode with my mother, who pulled me close, kissed my forehead, and gently said, "Your father calls me that out of love, my dear. There's no insult in his words."

"But how can mocking someone's waist be an act of love?" I retorted, bewildered.

"One day, when you grow older, you will understand the beauty and meaning in his words. Let's leave it at that for now," she said with a smile.

To humor me, my father promised, "Alright, from now on, I'll call her *"Beautiful-waisted one"*. Does that satisfy you?"

I nodded in agreement, and the matter ended there. But the memory lingered, and its significance unfolded with time.

As I grew into adolescence, I began to encounter beauty in its myriad forms. The world around me seemed filled with enchanting revelations—people, places, and emotions I'd never noticed before.

Many admired me, and some even expressed their love, but I found myself unable to choose a companion. To me, everyone seemed beautiful and deserving.

Then came Valentine's Day, a day of celebration among my peers. Couples gathered in a lush flower garden, their joy palpable. Alone, I sat on a raised platform, observing the scene below.

It was as if celestial beings had descended onto the earth—a divine assembly of lovebirds. The garden came alive with vibrant colors, laughter, and harmony. Love radiated from each pair, their faces glowing as if touched by divine light.

Each couple seemed lost in their own world, their movements synchronized like a graceful dance. Some playfully tied delicate flower garlands around each other's waists, pulling gently as their partners swayed with elegant charm. The waists of these women, slender and supple, moved with such fluidity that they seemed to embody the very essence of grace.

As dusk fell, the garden emptied, and everyone left with their hearts full of joy. The beauty and harmony I had witnessed lingered in my mind, echoing through my thoughts as I returned home.

That night, as I lay in bed, the scenes of the garden replayed before my eyes. The sway of those elegant waists stayed with me, lulling me into a dream. In that dream, my mother appeared—not as just my mother, but as a radiant figure surpassing all earthly beauty.

Her voice, like a soothing melody, whispered profound truths into my ears. She spoke of mysteries I had never fathomed—truths about creation, life, and the essence of being.

She revealed that her waist was not merely a part of her body but a sacred symbol:

- A cradle of life, the origin of our existence, and the sanctum of creation.

- A bridge of time, connecting the past to the present and guiding us toward the future.

- A foundation of strength, enabling us to rise to any height in life.

She explained that her steps had taught us to walk, her embrace had shielded us from storms, and her heart had filled our lives with love and blessings. Her waist, slender yet resilient, symbolized the balance and grace that carried us through life.

In that moment of revelation, I understood the profound beauty in my father's affectionate words. It was not mockery but reverence, a playful acknowledgment of the sacred role my mother's being played in shaping our lives.

Awakening from that dream, I realized that my mother's beauty was not just in her appearance but in her essence. She was the embodiment of love, grace, and selflessness—a sanctuary where we could always find refuge. Her every gesture, every touch, carried the power to nurture and guide.

The world may offer countless marvels, but the truest beauty lies in the unwavering love of a mother. Her form is a divine refuge, her being a source of inspiration, and her essence a melody that resonates in every heartbeat.

To honor and cherish her is not just a duty—it is the highest Law of our lives.

—·—·—●—·—·—

The Elegant Gift

Two extraordinary moments converged on a single day: my birthday and the day I assumed the role of CEO. One marked the origin of my life, and the other, the pinnacle of my progress and achievements. The day was made even more special by my mother's presence alongside my wife and children, sharing in my joy.

That morning was a medley of blessings, love, and admiration. My mother's warmth, my wife's devotion, and my children's affection enveloped me like a soothing cocoon, filling my heart with boundless happiness.

After soaking in the familial bliss, I headed to the office, where I was greeted with an overwhelming reception. My colleagues, from senior executives to the staff who kept our spaces clean, came together to honor my success. Their heartfelt admiration, reflected in their kind words and gestures, brought tears to my eyes. Humbled by their love, I embraced each one, expressing my gratitude.

Taking my seat in the CEO's chair for the first time felt surreal, as if the weight of countless aspirations had crystallized into that moment. Surrounded by applause and well-wishes, I felt gratitude toward the divine, my parents, and the organization that had nurtured me. I resolved to lead with integrity and purpose, honoring the trust placed in me.

That evening, a warm celebration awaited me at home. My wife had organized a beautiful gathering, complete with gifts from her and the children. Each token of love brought smiles and laughter, leaving me brimming with joy. Exhausted but content, I knelt before my mother, seeking her blessings before retiring to bed.

As I lay down, reflecting on the day's events, my daughter approached me with a curious question. "Papa, we all gave you gifts for your birthday, and even your office celebrated you becoming the CEO with flowers and praise. But why didn't grandma give you a gift? Why did she only bless you with empty hands?"

The innocent inquiry startled me. My daughter's question held a depth I had not considered. For a moment, I didn't know how to respond. Smiling gently, I said, "My dear, she gave me the greatest gift of all—my very life. What gift could surpass that?"

Though I tried to explain, my daughter seemed unconvinced. Dissatisfied with my answer, she turned away, leaving me to my thoughts. As sleep eluded me, I found myself grappling with a new question.

Why doesn't my mother ever give me a gift? Not now, not ever. Why does she withhold acknowledgment even when I achieve something noteworthy?

The memory of my daughter's question unsettled me. As I glanced at the pile of presents on the table, a small, empty space caught my attention. Was that space reserved for a gift my mother never gave? Tossing and turning, I realized I wasn't just questioning her actions—I was questioning my own understanding of her love.

The next morning, clarity dawned upon me. My doubts now seemed immature, my expectations misplaced. My mother was, and had always been, the ultimate gift. She didn't need to give me presents because she *was* the embodiment of everything I could ever need.

She had taught me to nurture love for others, to shoulder their burdens with patience, and to offer comfort to those in pain. She showed me how to melt my heart into compassion, to let kindness flow like a gentle stream. My mother instilled in me the values of humility, generosity, and the joy of bringing light into the lives of others.

Through her silent sacrifices, she became the foundation of my life. Without her guidance, how could I have forged meaningful relationships, earned respect, or even built a family that loves me deeply?

The realization humbled me. My earlier thoughts felt naive, and I silently apologized to my mother. Her gift wasn't tangible; it was the countless lessons and the unshakable love that shaped me into who I am today.

Walking into my office that morning, I carried with me a renewed sense of purpose—and a deep, abiding gratitude for the eternal gift of my mother.

The Beauty of Labor

One day, an intriguing conversation unfolded between my friend and me about the essence of a beautiful life. My friend eloquently shared his perspective, concluding that a joyful life is indeed a beautiful one. Yet, his words left me pondering a deeper question: *What truly constitutes a joyful life?*

My friend explained his view:

"A beautiful life is one where the house is brimming with laughter from children, wealth overflows, and there is no scarcity of food. There should be ample servants, ready to fulfill every command without question, and companions who agree with every word you say. The garage should be filled with luxury cars, relatives should visit frequently to brighten your home, and friends should surround you in abundance. Such a life would surely be beautiful and full of joy."

His vision of life was enticing, painting a picture of abundance and ease. But doubts crept into my mind. Would these truly lead to a joyful and beautiful life? I asked him:

"What happens when the children grow up, build their own families, and drift away? What if wealth, as fleeting as it is, slips through our fingers? If the servants rebel and leave, if relatives sever ties, or if friends turn foes—what then? Will life still be beautiful when these pillars crumble? Will the joy once felt linger forever?"

My questions left my friend silent, unable to offer clarity. We parted ways, each lost in thought. As I walked home, I continued questioning myself, engaging in an inner dialogue.

I wondered about the hermits living peacefully in solitude, the ancestors who journeyed vast lands without modern comforts, and the common folk who lived humbly but independently. Were these lives not beautiful? Were they devoid of joy?

True joy, I realized, must be everlasting. Fulfillment should be attainable. These are rare treasures, challenging to find. Yet, I pondered whether the beauty inherent in nature exists in life as well. Is beauty merely what pleases the eyes, or is it what stirs the soul?

Is the carefree existence of animals and birds more beautiful than the turbulent lives of humans? This question echoed in my mind, and my intellect offered no answers.

What defines beauty? Is it wealth, or is it something else? If wealth brings joy, does it inherently possess beauty? If so, what constitutes beauty? Is there an immutable, eternal beauty within our reach?

As these thoughts consumed me, the images of my parents danced vividly in my mind. Were they embodiments of beauty and wealth? Their way of life unfolded like a film before my eyes.

They would rise before dawn, as if their awakening stirred the blooming of lotuses and the chirping of birds. Their footsteps seemed to set the rhythm of nature itself.

Their day began with labor—one working for the family's security, the other for its beauty. They moved as shadows and companions, constantly supporting each other. Their toil was not burdensome; it was a joyful dance of life. In this dance, each claimed half the victory, sharing the rest with one another and their children. My mother poured half of her love into me, while my father shared half of his affection.

Where else could such unparalleled beauty and wealth be found? The sacrifices and labor of parents for their children are unmatched in their splendor. Work is beauty; Contentment is beauty;

Having no material desires is beauty; Loving and sharing is beauty. Life full of these beauties is the life full of joy.

A life of labor carries no burdensome worries. A life of rest lacks peace. It is in labor that one finds true and enduring joy. The laborer is always rich in spirit. This is a wealth that remains unshaken, a beauty that stands eternal.

Animals and birds know only to cherish and trust in labor. Only humans, who often shun labor and crave rest, fail to see life's true beauty. Instead, they chase illusions, lamenting endlessly when they fail to grasp the profound joy hidden in the simplicity of honest work.

The Steps that moved the Soul

When I was sixteen, my school hosted a drawing competition. My friends insisted I participate, encouraging me by calling me a deeply sensitive artist and pushing me forward with enthusiasm.

Truth be told, I wasn't particularly skilled at drawing. I was a jack of all trades and master of none—a fact only I was aware of. I could sketch small flowers, fruits, plants, and mountains, but I lacked any remarkable expertise. Nevertheless, it was a competition, and winning felt like an uphill battle. Still, my friends motivated me, and I didn't want to let them down.

I joined the competition with nothing more than a pencil in hand. Looking around, I saw everyone armed with colorful pencils and brushes, their faces brimming with confidence. They seemed lost in thought, their fingers twirling in the air as if painting their imaginations. Meanwhile, my nervousness was written all over me.

I wasn't there to win, but my friends' expectations weighed on me. Taking a deep breath, I prepared to start drawing.

At first, I had no idea what to draw. I sat for a while, restless and unsure, ruining and discarding four or five blank sheets in the process. Suddenly, a spark of inspiration lit up my mind, and I began drawing.

While others were still battling with their brushes, I finished my piece. Feeling proud, I congratulated myself and was convinced that I had created something exceptional. Surely, I thought, this would win an award.

Looking around, I saw others absorbed in their work, appearing like master poets creating visual symphonies. Their papers were alive with vibrant colors, while mine stood out in its stark black and white. But just as a nightingale doesn't need vibrant plumage to captivate, I believed in the strength of my emotions. I submitted my drawing to the judges with a hopeful heart and stepped out.

My friends immediately surrounded me, eager to know what I had drawn. "A truly meaningful piece," I said confidently. They were surprised to see that I had worked with nothing but a pencil. "No colors? No brushes?" they asked, astonished.

"Do shadows have colors? Does the sky? Do pupils or a girl's beautiful hair have colors? Let's move on," I replied, brushing aside their doubts.

That evening, the results were announced. I didn't win a prize. My drawing was deemed ineligible and set aside. I felt utterly disheartened, on the verge of tears.

"We told you before—can there be art without colors? Colors give life to drawings! You entered the competition with misplaced confidence but couldn't even hide your fear from us," my friends scolded.

"Not winning is fine," I said, "but declaring my work ineligible feels insulting. It was a deeply emotional piece. At least they could have acknowledged that."

"What emotion? Dark shadows, black pupils, black hair, black pencil strokes—is this your emotion?" they mocked.

"You encouraged me to participate, and now that I've lost, you're ridiculing me. Are you true friends? Never mind—I'll go back and meet the judges. I'll get to the bottom of this," I declared and walked back with determination.

The judges were still seated, deep in conversation. I approached them and gathered all the courage I could muster. Perhaps it was the courage born of failure. I asked them why my drawing was deemed ineligible.

They pulled out my work and laid it before me. "What is this?" they asked, raising their eyebrows. "These steps that begin in one corner and ascend diagonally—what are they? What do they mean? And what are these tiny steps beside them? Where is the beauty in this? How does this deserve to be eligible? Explain."

I took a deep breath and began, "These are a mother's steps. My mother's steps. Your mother's steps. The steps of all mothers. They guide us toward our goals, illuminating our path as they climb higher and higher. The tiny footprints beside them are mine, yours, and everyone else's—symbolizing the journey of children who follow in their mother's footsteps.

When we follow a mother's steps, there's no failure, no stumbling, no misstep. A mother ensures her children never falter. Her steps guide us through the dark, leading us to light and fulfilling our dreams. What beauty can surpass the grace of a mother's steps? They are sacred and deserve to be cherished, revered, and celebrated forever."

Moved by my explanation, the judges declared, "Your drawing deserves a special prize." Their kind words lifted my spirits and made my steps lighter as I walked way with a heart full of gratitude.

The Supreme Radiance

It was a stormy night, with relentless rain pouring down and strong winds howling outside. It was late, and I sat inside with my parents, the doors shut tightly against the storm. Thunder roared, and lightning flashed, but the rain showed no sign of stopping.

Suddenly, we heard loud knocking at the door. The sound was urgent and persistent. My mother got up to open it. Standing there was a man, drenched to the bone, shivering from head to toe. He was a stranger, someone we'd never seen before.

Without hesitation, my mother invited him inside. He stepped in gratefully, water dripping from his clothes, and she quickly shut the door behind him.

"Forgive me for intruding," he said, his voice trembling. "I was caught in the storm and couldn't find shelter. Could I stay here for a while?"

My mother's heart melted. She led him to the inner room, offering him warmth and comfort. Watching this unfold, I felt uneasy. Who was this man? What if he had ill intentions? He was tall, broad-shouldered, and intimidating—a complete stranger. Trusting him seemed reckless.

My father, however, sat calmly in his chair, sipping hot coffee, unaffected by my concerns. I voiced my worries, explaining that if this man were dangerous, we wouldn't stand a chance against him.

But my father remained unshaken. "Your mother is likely drying his hair with a towel right now," he remarked, smiling slightly.

Curious, I peeked into the other room. True to his words, my mother was gently drying the man's hair. I returned to my father, nodding in acknowledgment.

From his seat, my father began narrating, as if predicting the sequence of events. "She'll hand him towels to dry himself and give him dry clothes to wear. Then, she'll offer him hot coffee. Only when she sees him relax will she feel at ease."

Exactly as he described, my mother tended to the stranger. Her kindness and hospitality were boundless. Watching this, I couldn't contain my curiosity any longer and asked my father, "Why is she doing all this?"

"Because she's a mother," he said simply. "A mother's heart is unique. She sees her child in everyone. To her, that man was no stranger—he was you. A mother's love blinds her to differences and dangers. All she knows is how to nurture."

"But he's a stranger," I argued. "What if he intends harm?"

"A true child would never harm his mother," my father replied. "Deep down, every human shares the same heart. It mirrors the one they were born from. Open your heart like your mother does, and you'll see the whole world bathed in love."

My father's words struck me deeply. I had never heard him speak with such wisdom before. Usually, he was silent, like a vast ocean, imparting lessons without uttering a word. Yet, here he was, speaking profound truths about human nature and love.

As the storm subsided, I peered into the room again. My mother and the man were chatting warmly, as if they had known each other forever. Soon, he emerged, a changed man, gratitude shining in his eyes.

He turned to my mother and said, "Thank you, Dear. You reminded me of my own mother. In this short time, I felt as if I were home." He bowed respectfully to my father, then stepped outside, walking into the now-calm night.

I followed him to the door, watching as he disappeared into the distance. The storm had passed, and the sky was clear. The moon shone brightly, casting a serene glow over everything. Looking up at it, I felt a strange sense of peace.

As I stood there, lost in thought, I heard a voice call out, "Friend, wait!"

Startled, I turned around, but there was no one there. The voice called out again. This time, I looked up at the moon, and it felt as though it were speaking to me.

"Friend," it said, "you are fortunate. All this time, I thought I was the ultimate source of light, spreading my radiance over the world. But now I see how insignificant I am. Unlike me, who wanes and disappears, a mother's light shines constantly. She never dims, never falters. Her love and care are endless, as if she were the true full moon."

The moon paused, as if reflecting on its own words, then continued, "Tonight, I learned that mothers are the real beacons of light, and their children are the blossoms of that light. If I were to have another birth, I would wish to be a mother, or at least be born as a child to one."

The voice faded, leaving me overwhelmed with emotion. My eyes filled with tears as I gazed at the luminous moon, its light now holding a deeper meaning.

The Fulfilled Soul

One day, I visited a temple. I was warmly welcomed and given a divine darshan. The priests performed grand rituals and blessed me with Vedic chants. They wished for me to flourish as a *"a fulfilled person"*.

Next, I visited a church. There, compassionate hearts greeted me with open arms, offering prayers on my behalf. They shared messages of peace and imparted sacred teachings, blessing me to live a *"complete life."*

Later, I went to a mosque. With hearts full of love, they embraced me and invited me inside. They showered me with boundless affection, taught me the principles of virtuous living, and blessed me to lead a *"wholesome life."*

Enveloped in divine experiences, I returned home, feeling as though waves of spiritual energy were carrying me. The path I walked every day felt fresh, brimming with newfound wonder.

Back at home, I sat peacefully, reflecting on the blessings and wisdom I had received. My body felt weightless, and my mind seemed to soar in the vast sky. The words of blessings echoed in my heart, forming a triangle of meaning in my thoughts: *fulfilled life, complete life, wholesome life.*

Yet, questions began to stir within me. What did these blessings truly mean? What was the essence of each? Why were they phrased differently, even though their core seemed identical? Why did differences in expressions divide people? If the essence of religion is the well-being of humanity, why are there conflicts between faiths? Why do divisions, violence, and hatred exist?

These questions weighed heavily on my heart, and I began to feel a growing sadness.

What does it mean to be a *fulfilled person*? How does one achieve a *complete* or *wholesome* life? Does this require education, wealth, or something else entirely? Are there truly any *fulfilled* people in this world? If so, who are they?

I turned to elders and scholars for answers, but they spoke only of figures from ancient times. They painted the past as a golden age, yet said nothing about the present.

Then I thought, *What about my mother?* Could she hold the answers I sought? I decided to ask her, trusting her wisdom to guide me.

"Mother," I began, "what does it mean to live a fulfilled life? Who is a *fulfilled person?*"

Surprised, she asked, "Did you come all this way just to ask me that?"

"I tried elsewhere, Mother, but found no satisfying answers. You know how restless my curiosity makes me. Please, calm my mind."

As all mothers do, she embraced me with love and began to share her insights, her words brimming with the wisdom of the ages.

"A *fulfilled person,*" she said, "is one who remains humble no matter how high they rise in life. They are adorned with humility and never forget their roots.

"They reveal their knowledge and wisdom only when necessary, offering guidance to those in need without seeking recognition.

"They wear virtues as their garments, yet possess the strength to stand firm against vices. They shine with goodness, illuminating those around them.

"They live with constant joy, embracing life's joys and sorrows with a smile, never retreating in the face of hardship.

"They consider freedom from desires as true wealth. Even if they have desires, they channel them towards the betterment of the world, sacrificing their own needs for the greater good.

"They leave behind a legacy of love that endures even after their death, inspiring others through their deeds and actions.

"A *fulfilled person* wins the hearts of others with their compassion and loving nature, wielding virtue as their only weapon.

"Such a person, my child, is the embodiment of completeness. The blessings you received today carry this profound truth. It takes immense effort, dedication, and a willingness to shed material attachments to become such a person. But know this: it is possible for anyone, including you, to achieve this.

"With blessings and a determined heart, you can not only transform yourself but also inspire others to become *fulfilled souls.*"

Her words resonated deeply within me. They weren't just answers—they were a path, a guiding light. I bowed to her wisdom, feeling a newfound clarity and purpose. From that moment on, I resolved to strive towards becoming a *fulfilled person,* carrying the 'blessings' in my heart.

—·—·—●—·—·—

The Art and the Brilliance

I sat atop a towering peak, marveling at a magnificent sculpture before me. Its creator stood nearby, intently observing their masterpiece. I was awestruck—what beauty, what intricate art, and what radiant splendor!

Curious, I joined the sculptor in examining the artwork. As my gaze swept over the sculpture, each detail seemed to reveal itself as a living story.

First, I looked at the feet. They were delicate yet sturdy, exuding a golden glow, as soft as flower petals but strong enough to support the immense figure above. They were feet that walked with purpose, guiding themselves and others along the right path, ever moving toward a noble destination.

Then I saw the calves, firm and unyielding, like iron pillars supporting an immense structure. They symbolized relentless effort and industry, standing tall and unwavering.

The thighs reminded me of the branches of a vast, sheltering tree, offering shade and solace to anyone in need. They were strong and steady, embodying resilience and compassion for those weary from life's battles.

The waist was slim and agile, exuding youthful energy and grace. It stood as a testament to victories achieved and challenges overcome—a silent reminder of humility amidst success.

I noticed the navel, the deep source of life itself, connecting the sculpture to its origins. It was a sacred point, representing the womb from which all vitality flows.

Moving upward, I saw the chest, proud and expansive, a symbol of courage and achievement. The neck, tall and graceful, seemed crafted to voice declarations of triumph and to swallow life's sorrows with dignity. Around it glistened an ornament, a testament to the grandeur of life's accomplishments.

The shoulders were broad and powerful, capable of bearing the heaviest burdens. They radiated strength, a protective shield for the entire sculpture. The arms, muscular and poised, extended outward, ready to embrace the world or to shield against harm. The hands, with their five distinct fingers, were intricately detailed, resembling a snake's hood, prepared to act with precision.

The face was mesmerizing—a masterpiece of expression. Framed by flowing black hair resembling ocean waves, it sparkled with countless emotions and lights. The smile welcomed friends, while the victorious grin radiated confidence. I saw the innocence of youth, the wisdom of age, and the brilliance of love, care, and knowledge shining in its eyes and broad forehead.

As I closed my eyes, the entire sculpture came alive in my mind. It embodied the balance of the three gunas (virtues) — *tamas* (Ignorance), *rajas* (Passion), and *sattva* (Wisdom)—and stood as a timeless representation of the past, present, and future. It felt as though the sculpture was the universe itself, and the universe was the sculpture.

Who crafted this masterpiece? Who was this extraordinary sculptor?

In that moment of clarity, the truth struck me. The figure towering before me was my mother. The sculptor who had shaped this divine creation was also her—my mother.

But the vision went beyond her. The sculpture reflected the essence of every mother. All mothers are sculptors, tirelessly dedicating themselves to shaping their children into masterpieces. Their lives revolve around molding their children, delighting in their creations, and cherishing every detail they imbue with their love and care.

My mother had spent eighty years shaping me, giving her life and energy to make me who I am today. She placed me atop a high pedestal, ensuring I reached my potential. Even now, her aging eyes and wrinkled face meticulously examined me, searching for ways to refine me further. Though her hands trembled and her body tired, she still held the sculptor's chisel firmly.

The philosophy of mothers everywhere is clear: no matter how high their children ascend, they must continue to grow. For mothers, this is the ultimate fulfillment—to see their children evolve into their finest selves, to marvel at the beauty of their creation, and to take pride in the art and radiance they have infused into their children's lives.

The Soul Illumined

'Don't lie—it displeases God."

"Don't commit sins—God will punish you."

"Don't hurt others—it grieves God."

I grew up hearing countless such phrases. But who decides what is truth, sin, or wrongdoing? Isn't it other humans?

They say, "You can escape the law but not God." But who is this God? Where is He? What does He look like? If all living beings are His creation, why did He create flawed humans? How can a God, supposedly perfect and pure, have faults, anger, or favoritism? Why does He appear in human form if He governs the universe?

These questions swirled endlessly in my mind. If God governs everything, why does He allow flaws and imperfections? Why do we see Him in so many forms, and how do we know which is the true one? I longed to meet Him, to ask my questions directly, to understand the truth.

My endless curiosity made people mock me. "You'll go mad or renounce the world," they warned. "Why can't you just live without overthinking?" But their words couldn't bring me peace.

One day, I sought out my mother, hoping she would have the answers. Unlike others, she lived peacefully, speaking to birds, playing with animals, caressing flowers, and embracing trees. She even scattered grains for insects. To me, she seemed even more eccentric than I was. The difference was that while my mind was restless, hers radiated contentment.

I approached her hesitantly, ready to unburden my thoughts.

"Mother, who is God? What does He look like? Is He really the human-like figure we worship? Where does He live? Can we see Him, talk to Him? Please, answer me and ease my troubled mind!"

She listened calmly, her face adorned with a serene smile. Her eyes sparkled with the wisdom only a mother could possess. "Sit, my child," she said gently, her voice soothing like a lullaby. Then she began:

"God doesn't have a specific address, my dear. He is omnipresent, existing everywhere and within everyone. God isn't something you can see with your eyes, but you can feel His presence.

God and godliness are different. A person who loves is called a lover, and one who worships is called a devotee. Similarly, godliness refers to divine qualities—love, compassion, kindness, empathy, and selfless acts. These qualities are divine, whether they manifest in humans, animals, or even trees. That's why some cultures worship animals and nature—they recognize the divinity within them.

Both God and evil reside within you. Your heart is their shared home. If you awaken the divine within you, you become godly. If you awaken the demonic, you become a sinner. The choice is yours.

Every religion teaches us to nurture the divine within and destroy the demonic. Those who fail to realize this search for God in temples, mosques, and churches, not understanding that He resides within them.

To become divine, one must strive and practice. Godliness isn't given; it's earned. When everyone realizes this, the world will be full of gods. Until then, God remains hidden within us."

Her words illuminated my soul. I resolved to awaken the divine within me through devotion and dedication. I realized God has no form, but if He did, He would look like the Mother.

A mother's ability to bring life into the world is the greatest miracle of all. That miracle, that nurturing power, is God itself.

The Story of a Victor

In the initial days after my father's passing, I was overwhelmed by despair and hopelessness. My intellect and enthusiasm seemed to vanish, and my behavior changed drastically. This shift began to impact my professional and personal life. The company I had built with so much effort started incurring significant losses.

On the other hand, my mother chose to stay in our ancestral home, living alone. The sheer burden of the situation left her vulnerable, yet she remained calm. My family, observing my struggles, was disheartened.

I couldn't help but think of my mother. Despite having a family, I felt alone. Imagining her loneliness was unbearable. I decided to visit her.

When I arrived, I was surprised to see my mother as cheerful as ever. She appeared unaffected by the chaos in my life, living her days peacefully, exuding strength like an unshaken ocean amidst a storm.

I shared my struggles with her, expecting her to be distressed. But instead of showing sympathy, she gently asked, "Would you like to hear a story?"

I was taken aback. A story? At a time like this? "Mother, I don't need stories now. I need comfort," I said.

But she smiled knowingly. "Life itself is a story, my child. Every life event births stories. Within stories lie the truths of life. Listen carefully."

Reluctantly, I stayed quiet as she began.

"Once upon a time, there was a king. His queen was abducted by a demon and taken to a distant land. The king sent his trusted aide on a mission to rescue her. The aide reached the shore of a vast ocean, battled hundreds of demons, and found the queen's whereabouts. He assured her of her safety, returned to the king with the news, and together they launched an attack. They destroyed the demon's kingdom, reunited the king and queen, and established peace.

Do you know how the aide achieved this feat? He used his intellect, courage, and determination. With careful planning and unyielding bravery, he overcame formidable challenges. And above all, it was his unwavering resolve that carried him through. That's the story, my child."

I couldn't hide my confusion. "But why this story now, Mother?"

"Because life is full of challenges, my dear," she said. "Facing them with strength and moving forward is what makes someone truly human. Only those who rise above adversity will taste victory.

The greatest loss in life is not knowing the purpose of your existence. Losing sight of life's meaning is the ultimate defeat.

Your father would never want to see you lose hope. He would wish for you to live fully and fulfill your potential. If you crumble under despair, his soul will be burdened.

Birth and death are inevitable, but living as though dead is the worst curse.

Your father's dream was to see you succeed. If you accomplish that, his soul will rejoice. Like the hero in my story, arm yourself with determination, intellect, courage, and vision. Fight against despair and emerge victorious.

The past is gone, and the present is fleeting. All that remains is the future. Move forward, my child. Do not let sorrow hold you back.

Run alongside time, don't stand still. Stagnation only leads to further loss. Go forth, and success will be yours."

Her words lit a fire within me. I recognized my duty. To honor my father's memory and fulfill his wishes, I decided to walk the path of victory.

I glanced back at my mother as I left. She was smiling at me, her gaze steady and reassuring. Like the sun that conceals its fiery core to gift us light and warmth, like the moon that transforms harsh sunlight into gentle moonlight, she embodied strength and grace in its purest form.

Language of the Eyes

My mother, who was always cheerful, lively, and vibrant, fell gravely ill once. A severe throat ailment left her unable to speak or eat. The doctors concluded that surgery was the only solution.

The surgery was successful, but the doctors advised her not to speak for a week. The ever-chatty, melodious voice of my mother went silent. Her lips, which usually murmured Love and affection, now rested in stillness. It pained me deeply to see her like this.

My father and I stayed by her side during those days. The weight of worry etched itself onto our faces. Yet, my mother continued to smile, as radiant as ever. Her resilience amazed me.

My father never left her side, serving her with utmost dedication—offering medicines on time, attending to her every need, and responding to her smallest gestures. Witnessing their silent communication was nothing short of magical.

It struck me then: could there be another couple in the world as beautiful as them? The essence of Sacred bonding, where one exists for the other, unfolded before me in its purest form. Their love and devotion were truly awe-inspiring.

But one question lingered in my mind—how did my father understand my mother's needs without her saying a word? How could he anticipate and respond to her desires so seamlessly? Curious, I asked him, "Father, how do you know what she needs? How do you talk to her when she can't speak? What is the medium of your communication? I can't seem to understand."

My father smiled and gently ruffled my hair. "Son, when your mother resides in my heart and I in hers, what need is there for words? Our eyes do the talking," he said.

I was astonished. Could eyes possess such power? Could they speak volumes without words? Captivated by the thought, I spent the next few days observing my mother's eyes, hoping to uncover their mysteries.

In her eyes, I found boundless beauty—an unparalleled grace that only a sensitive soul could perceive. Her gaze was mesmerizing, a sight that made me want to look again and again.

Her eyes were filled with love, a vast ocean of affection that only a mother could possess. They overflowed with unconditional love that could envelop the entire creation in its warmth.

In those eyes, I saw compassion—a tenderness that could melt the hardest hearts, extinguish the fiercest flames, and calm the most turbulent storms. They could bind even the most unyielding souls with the soft chains of love.

Her gaze could inspire the despondent, fill the weak with courage, and transform the timid into the bold. Her eyes were like dark clouds, brimming with mercy, ready to shower kindness and empathy on those in need.

A mother's gaze holds the power to nurture a child into a complete individual, a force that shapes new creations. With just her glance, she can guide her children's steps, correct their paths, and communicate profound emotions without uttering a word.

Her eyes are the gateways to her soul, revealing her innermost self. They are divine, luminous, and vast.

As I delved deeper into the mystery of my mother's gaze, I discovered profound truths and secrets that surpassed my expectations. I realized that the beauty of a mother's eyes is an unparalleled treasure—a gift bestowed uniquely upon women, and most magnificently upon mothers.

When hearts are in sync, words become unnecessary. Eyes convey everything. They teach immutable truths while dancing with life.

Understanding the secrets in my mother's eyes, I felt blessed. I grasped the depth of love and connection between my parents. How divine are eyes that can speak without speaking!

As I turned to look at my mother, her eyes met mine. They sparkled with a radiant smile. Those eyes, her eyes, were speaking to me.

Yes, now I understood. My mother's eyes were saying, "Don't worry, my child. I'm getting better. I'll recover soon."

Even Distant, Still Near

Mother had written me a letter. She mentioned that Father had gone on a journey with his friends to a faraway place. He would be gone for fifteen days, she said, and asked if everyone here was doing well.

The tone of the letter puzzled me. Was she hinting for me to join her? Or was she planning to visit me? Or was it just a casual note to keep me informed? Knowing my mother, she never wrote letters without purpose, but what was she trying to convey?

I also knew she wasn't shy about visiting me unannounced. She had surprised me on several occasions in the past. Perhaps she was hesitating to bother me, knowing how caught up I usually am with my work.

Mother and Father had always been inseparable. The idea of her being alone for fifteen days felt unsettling. I recalled how, years ago, when Mother went to her hometown, Father became restless and could hardly bear her absence.

I, too, had once experienced the agony of separation when my wife and children were away for an extended period. I couldn't last long without them and went to bring them back.

Surely, Mother must be feeling lonely without Father. For all the sacrifices she's made for me, the least I could do was set aside my work and visit her. I decided to go, without informing her, to surprise her and keep her company.

When I arrived at her home, I gently pushed open the door. There she was, sitting quietly and reading a book. The moment she saw me, her face lit up with surprise and joy. She stood up, came over, and embraced me warmly.

She made me sit down and fussed over me, asking about everyone's well-being. Her happiness was evident, and I felt a sense of fulfillment for having made the trip.

We spent hours chatting, catching up on little things. Suddenly, she called me for lunch, saying, "Come, let's eat."

I was taken aback. How had she managed to prepare lunch without leaving my side?

"Mother, did you already cook? Did you know I was coming? How is that possible?" I asked, astonished.

"Since morning, there have been signs, son," she replied with a smile. "The breeze felt new, as if carrying a message. Birds sang by the windows, and the calf in the yard kept calling out as if announcing something. Even my coffee tasted different today. I felt as though I wasn't walking on the ground but floating. I sensed that someone dear was coming. And who could that be if not you?"

Her words touched my heart deeply. Tears welled up in my eyes as I bent to touch her feet, thanking her for the love she showered on me.

Later, as we sat down for a meal, I couldn't help but notice how much tastier the food seemed that day. It wasn't just her hands that had prepared it—it was her heart.

After we finished, Mother looked at me and asked, "Son, what brings you here? Is there something special?"

Her question surprised me. Didn't she remember writing to me? Wasn't that why I had come?

"Mother, didn't you write to me? I came because of your letter. Father is away for fifteen days, and I thought you might feel lonely, so I came to keep you company."

"Oh, my dear, I didn't call you. I only wrote to inform you, nothing more. But hearing you say you came for me fills my heart with joy. Won't your work suffer? Won't your family miss you? Is it okay for you to stay here?"

"Mother," I said, "the world won't collapse without me. Who else matters more to me than you? Even my wife insisted I come. Everyone knows how much you mean to us."

She smiled warmly. "I'm so glad you came, son. But you must know, I am never truly alone. Let me tell you a story, one that inspires me."

She began narrating a tale, her words filled with wisdom as always.

"Once, there was a princess who was married to a prince. Due to unforeseen circumstances, they were exiled to the forest. One day, while the prince was away, a demon abducted the princess and took her far away to his island.

The prince sent a messenger to find her. After a long and arduous journey, the messenger located the princess. He asked her, 'Isn't it hard for you to be away from your husband for so long?'

The princess replied, 'My heart is with him, and his heart is with me. How can we ever be apart? No matter where we are, we are always together.'"

Mother concluded, "She is my inspiration, son. Even though your father may be physically far away, he is always with me, just as I am with him. When hearts are bound, distance doesn't matter."

Her words resonated deeply within me. I understood the divine bond between my parents and the love they shared. From that moment on, they became my ultimate role models.

—·—·—●—·—·—

Restless Yet Content

Father was busy harvesting crops in the field. I wanted to join him, and Mother decided to come along as well. She packed a cart full of delicious food for Father, ensuring every detail was taken care of. Together, we set out to meet him.

We own a ten-acre farmland, and during the harvest season, Father rarely comes home. He sometimes spends nights in the fields, overseeing the work. That's why, occasionally, Mother and I visit him to spend time together.

When we arrived, we saw him working alongside the laborers, bending over the lush green crops with determination. Father always loved working shoulder-to-shoulder with the workers, finding joy in labor. Seeing us, he brightened up and gestured for us to sit under a shady tree.

Mother and I sat in the shade, watching the workers sing songs in unison as they toiled away, forgetting the fatigue of their labor. After about half an hour, Father joined us. Mother lovingly served him the food she had prepared, feeding him until he was full. After chatting with us briefly, he returned to the field.

Watching Mother and Father filled me with admiration. Both were tireless in their efforts—Mother managing the home and Father protecting it. Together, they worked for my happiness. They were the embodiment of dedication, and I, their fortunate child, enjoyed the fruits of their labor.

"Father won't be done anytime soon," Mother said, snapping me out of my thoughts. "Let's take a stroll through the grove."

We entered the grove, a two-acre plot that Father had transformed into a lush artificial forest.

"If we had planted crops here instead of trees, we could have earned a lot more," I remarked, looking at the flourishing plants, chirping birds, and grazing animals around us.

"This isn't just a forest, my dear. It's a beautiful grove your father created for me," Mother replied with a smile. "When I walk here, your father feels as if his heart is dancing with joy. Isn't it enough that the three of us live peacefully? Wealth has no end, but it doesn't bring contentment."

Her words struck a chord with me. I took her hand, and together we wandered through the grove.

The grove seemed to come alive with Mother's presence, radiating a newfound beauty. Birds flapped their wings, eager to perch on her shoulders and head, chirping joyfully. Even the fledglings in their nests sang welcome songs to her.

The trees swayed their branches as if performing a divine dance. The gentle breeze played with her hair, carrying whispers of affection. The brook slowed its flow as if reluctant to move past her, murmuring its admiration.

Cows and calves ran toward her, trying to nuzzle her cheeks but falling short. Mother knelt to pet them lovingly, her affection evident in every gesture.

She wandered over to touch the motionless trees and plants, as if consoling them for their inability to come to her. She playfully sprinkled water from the brook and caressed the flowers. Exhausted from the day's activities, she turned to me with a contented smile.

"I'm tired, son. Let's rest under my favorite tree," she said, guiding me toward a tall, sturdy tree.

"Why is this tree your favorite, Mother?" I asked curiously.

"This tree was planted by your father with his own hands. It has grown into a magnificent tree, providing us with shade and solace. Even when struck by stones, it gives sweet fruit. Even when its branches are cut, it sprouts anew. That's why I cherish it," she explained, her voice filled with reverence.

Mother laid her head in my lap, saying she would rest for a while. Moments later, she drifted into a peaceful sleep, her serene face graced by an everlasting smile.

Nature seemed to pause around her. Dark clouds gathered above, providing shade for her rest. The wind softened its pace, rustling gently through her hair. Flowers fell to the ground, releasing their fragrance into the air. The brook's usual babble turned into a soothing murmur. Birds quieted their chirps, whispering softly among themselves. Even the calves ceased their frolic and lay down.

All these changes appeared to be in reverence to Mother's presence. How wondrous it was! Could nature respond so beautifully to love? Could it reciprocate affection so magnificently?

This was the essence of motherhood—boundless love that embraced all beings. If only we could love as mothers do, wouldn't the entire creation transform into a childlike innocence, radiating joy?

As I sat there, gazing at Mother's serene face, her innocence and purity shone through. She lay in my lap, her hair swaying gently in the breeze, and I could not take my eyes off her. The world around seemed to pause, as if to savor the love that emanated from her. I, too, was mesmerized, basking in the divine presence of my Mother.

—·—·—●—·—·—·—

Birthdays

During my childhood, I once attended a celebration at my friend's house. It was his mother's birthday, and their family, being well-off, had organized a grand event, inviting everyone from the neighborhood. My mother and I were among the guests.

My friend's father had great affection for his family and spared no effort in making the celebration a grand affair. A sumptuous feast was arranged, which everyone enjoyed with delight.

My friends and I spent the day playing games and singing songs. Everyone, including the children, received gifts. My friend then turned to me and said, "Let's celebrate your mother's birthday with equal grandeur! We'll have so much fun."

I nodded in agreement.

"When's your mother's birthday, by the way?" he asked.

With pride, I replied, "My mother and I share the same birthday!"

He burst into laughter and teased, "How's that possible? Your mom's older than you! If both of you were born on the same day, then wouldn't she have to come to school with us too?"

I was puzzled by his question. It did seem odd, but I had no answer. His laughter and question lingered in my mind, and I couldn't stop thinking about it.

After the celebration, Mother and I returned home, but his question followed us like a shadow. At home, Mother joyfully described the festivities to my father, recounting every detail. Once she finished, I hesitantly asked my question.

Both my parents exchanged a smile, amused by my innocence. Father affectionately ruffled my hair and walked away. But I persisted, repeatedly asking Mother for an explanation.

Finally, one day, Mother sat me down and shared words that left a lasting impression on me—words that deepened my respect for women. Her response remains etched in my memory, and even today, it resonates with a profound significance.

"Son," she began, "I don't have just one birthday—I have many. Every single one is a celebration in its own way.

The moment life began to form within me, that was my first birthday—a miraculous moment beyond imagination. Though I had no shape, no form, I was alive within my mother's womb, growing, sharing her breath and her hunger.

Nine months later, as I emerged into the world, bringing my mother immense pain, I experienced another birth. That was the day I first touched the earth, breathed on my own, and became an independent being.

As I grew, crawling, playing, and laughing, I crossed from childhood into adolescence. My body underwent changes, and one day, I experienced the cycle of womanhood for the first time. It brought discomfort but was celebrated by everyone. They gathered and rejoiced, calling it a milestone in my life—a day that marked another birth for me.

As the years went by, society imposed restrictions on me, drawing lines I couldn't cross. I was no longer allowed to mingle freely or play as I once did. Finally, my marriage to your father marked another birth—the day I became a wife, left my parental home, and stepped into a new chapter of life.

With your father, I experienced the sweetness of life, the joy of companionship, and the richness of love. Then came the day you were conceived within me—a day of immense happiness that brought another birth. For nine months, you were a part of me, and when you were born, I endured the pain of labor, teetering on the edge of life and death. Yet, your arrival made me feel reborn. That day, your birthday, was also my rebirth as a mother.

Of all these days, which one do you think is my true birthday? I cannot say. But I have chosen the day you entered my life as the one that truly defines me—the day I became a mother. Every other day fades in comparison to the joy you brought me. That is why your birthday is my greatest celebration—the day I became complete, the day I became a mother."

Her words revealed a profound truth about life and motherhood. As I grew older, their depth became even clearer. It is because of those words that my respect for women has only grown stronger, and it will remain so, forever.

—•—•—◆—•—•—

The Lost Address

One day, I was traveling to my hometown by car, accompanied by a driver. Sitting alone in the back seat, I gazed at the trees rushing past, their movement seemingly in reverse as the car sped ahead.

As we passed through a picturesque valley, the car suddenly came to a halt. The driver informed me that the car had broken down and would take about half an hour to fix.

I stepped out, told the driver to call me when it was ready, and began walking along the road. I absorbed the natural beauty around me, marveling at the serene surroundings. Soon, I spotted a small hill and decided to climb it for a better view.

From the hilltop, I saw a quaint village nestled in the valley below. Women carrying pots filled with water walked in a rhythmic procession, their steps graceful and purposeful. A group of men herded cattle toward the fields, their movements brisk.

Beyond the village, a large pond shimmered in the sunlight. Children splashed and swam, their laughter echoing through the still air. The village itself was a cluster of traditional clay-roofed houses, and the entire scene was bathed in the golden glow of the sun, which seemed to embrace the land with warmth.

The trees swayed gently, their branches alive with chirping birds building nests. Farmers on bicycles rode past, their baskets brimming with fresh vegetables. The soft breeze carried a new vitality, filling my lungs with freshness and my heart with joy.

As I stood there, mesmerized, a voice broke through my reverie: "Are you from the city, sir?"

I turned to see an elderly man with a white beard, wearing a traditional turban and holding a long staff. His clothes were as bright and clean as freshly bloomed jasmine.

"Yes, how did you know?" I asked, intrigued.

"You look different," he replied with a gentle smile. "You're well-dressed but seem restless. Your face carries tension, and though you're admiring the village, there's an impatience in your movements. Such people are usually from the city. I guessed and confirmed by observing you closely."

I was amazed by his sharp observation and intelligence.

"Yes, my car broke down, so I decided to explore while it's being repaired. I must say, your village is beautiful, and the atmosphere here is refreshing," I said.

Just then, the driver called to inform me that the car was ready. As I prepared to leave, the old man handed me two freshly picked fruits.

"Always keep a smile on your face, sir. That is the real address of a man," he said, his voice echoing wisdom.

The car resumed its journey, and the sweet fragrance of the fruits filled the cabin. They were as delightful as the man's words. I thought to myself, *I should take these to my mother; she'll be happy.*

As I leaned back, his words lingered in my ears: *A smile is a person's true address.*

Thoughts swirled in my mind. It was true—smiles had become rare in our city lives. Amid the hustle and bustle, we had lost the simplicity and authenticity of rural life.

In the city, everyone seemed burdened by stress and anxiety. Smiles, when they appeared, were often artificial or fleeting. Conversations were hurried, relationships transactional, and genuine human connections scarce.

My mother's words echoed in my mind: *Desires and ambitions weigh people down, making them forget the simple joys of life. In the race to achieve more, people overlook the peace and contentment that come from within.*

Finally, I reached my village. As my large car rolled into the narrow lanes, villagers stopped and stared with curiosity and amazement. Among these simple, genuine people, I felt like a stranger—an outsider.

When I arrived home, my mother was waiting for me at the door, her face lit with a radiant smile.

At that moment, I realized that the address I thought I had lost was never far away—it was right here, in my mother's smile. It was the most beautiful and comforting sight I had ever known.

The Power of Tenderness

Near our home, there lived a peculiar woman with a unique personality. She harbored an intense desire to outshine everyone in every aspect. She could not tolerate even the slightest success of others. Consumed by jealousy and resentment, she viewed everyone as her enemy.

In contrast, my mother had no enemies in the neighborhood or even the entire village. She treated everyone with love, greeted them with a warm smile, and forged friendships effortlessly. Even strangers would be drawn to her charm and warmth, becoming her admirers. Yet, this neighbor could not bring herself to like my mother. She envied my mother's radiance and resented her.

She constantly tried to emulate my mother, mimicking her behavior and mannerisms, hoping to gain the same affection and respect. Despite her efforts, she could not match even a fraction of my mother's grace. This deepened her jealousy and filled her with an unrelenting bitterness.

The woman even created a garden, much like my mother's. She planted various flowers and fruit trees, watering them diligently in the hope of seeing them flourish. However, her impatience and frustration grew as the plants failed to bloom or bear fruit. In contrast, my mother's garden thrived, brimming with vibrant flowers and fragrant fruits, a testament to her loving care.

Birds that were fed grains by the neighbor would eat and then fly to my mother's garden, joining the other birds in playful harmony. This made her furious. Over time, she alienated even her husband with her constant complaints and bitterness, becoming a source of fear and discomfort for everyone around her.

One day, she came to our home. My mother welcomed her warmly, offering her a seat and treating her with kindness. Despite my mother's hospitality, the woman was seething with anger and began speaking harshly.

"Why does everyone in the village despise me? Why does no one acknowledge me as they do you? What do you have that I don't? I have more wealth than you, yet I receive no respect! My garden wilts, my flowers fade before blooming, and my trees dry up before bearing fruit. Even animals shy away from me. What wrong have I done? Why does everyone love you but hate me? I can't bear this anymore. The pain is too much to handle. Why is this happening to me?" she vented, trembling with rage and sorrow.

My mother, unfazed by her outburst, gently drew her close, wiping away her tears and offering comfort. Slowly, the woman calmed down, her anger giving way to vulnerability. Like a child eager to learn, she listened intently as my mother spoke.

"Sister, your suffering is not your fault. It's the result of the negativity that has taken root in your heart, overshadowing the love, kindness, and compassion that naturally reside within you. These dark forces have suppressed the light of your heart, but it's still there. If you nurture it, your inner light can illuminate the world.

Life's happiness lies in contentment, in living without comparisons, and in embracing love. Begin by appreciating your husband. Speak to him with love, and you will see how he thrives under your affection and returns it to you a hundredfold. Happiness isn't found elsewhere; it resides within you and your home. Let go of your bitterness and embrace your duties as a wife and a mother. When you experience the love of being a mother, your world will transform into a temple of love."

The woman left with my mother's blessings, laden with fruits and gifts. Over time, she embraced my mother's words, uprooting the negativity within her. Love became her guiding force, and she transformed into a figure of compassion. Within a year, she gave birth to a healthy child, becoming a mother. From that moment on, her demeanor changed entirely. She loved and was loved in return.

Her once barren garden now thrived with new life. Flowers blossomed, trees sprouted fresh leaves, and birds built nests in her sanctuary. The fragrance of her flowers and the sweetness of her fruits mirrored the love that now filled her heart. Her life, once steeped in bitterness, became a fragrant celebration of motherhood and love.

The Rolling Tears

I had to travel to another town for an important office assignment. A hotel room was arranged for me. After completing my first day's work, I returned to the hotel in the evening. It wasn't dark yet. After a quick shower, I sat on the balcony with a cup of coffee, gazing at the bustling road below, filled with the noise of passing vehicles.

Across the road, directly opposite me, stood a large building. The signboard at its entrance read: "Old Age Home." The sight piqued my curiosity. Who are these elderly people? Where did they come from? I wondered. Just then, the waiter came to collect my empty coffee cup, and I asked him.

"That's a large old age home, sir. It houses nearly a hundred elderly residents. It's run with the help of generous donors. The facilities there are excellent, and the staff are dedicated and compassionate. It is managed by a Swamiji. A nominal fee is collected for maintenance," he explained.

"Are they all abandoned orphans? Do they gather people from the streets and take care of them?" I asked.

The waiter chuckled. "Not at all, sir. If they were all orphans, who would pay the fees? These are people from well-to-do families. Their children are too busy with jobs or businesses to look after them, so they leave them here and visit occasionally. Some come once in a while, while others, being extremely busy, don't come at all."

I was astonished. My expression must have betrayed my thoughts, as the waiter continued, "Why are you surprised, sir? The world has changed, and so have people. Everyone's focus is on earning money. Love and relationships no longer hold the same value. Tomorrow is a special day—the annual Parents' Day. All their children will come to visit."

With that, he left the room, leaving me alone with my thoughts. I paced back and forth, burdened by the questions swirling in my mind. What should I feel—pity or anger—when I see the changing world around me? Unlike humans, animals and birds never change their way of life with passing generations. Why are humans breaking the bonds of family and running toward materialistic desires? It felt as if humanity had lost its anchor, like a kite with a broken string or a rudderless boat.

For some time, I sat down, overwhelmed by these thoughts. That night, I couldn't eat properly. My mind wandered to my mother. She was a queen in her own right—independent and composed. She had carved paths for my future when I was still a child. Always joyful, my mother had lived with a steadfastness that I deeply admired. She never depended on anyone for support. Her constant joy was her secret to good health, and her unwavering contentment was her breath of life. She was like a lotus in a pond—living in the water yet untouched by it.

What happens to those who cannot live like her? Is this their fate in their final days?

I eagerly awaited the next day to observe the old age home and the families visiting their elderly. Eventually, I drifted into a restless sleep.

The next morning, I got ready and sat on the balcony, eagerly watching the old age home. The elderly residents bustled with excitement, dressed beautifully, awaiting their loved ones. One by one, the families started arriving. Soon, the entire home was abuzz with activity, children running around and families laughing together.

Fruits, sweets, and various goodies were distributed among the elderly, bringing smiles to their faces. Cameras clicked as families captured happy moments, creating memories. A politician arrived, greeted the residents, and delivered a long speech before leaving in his car.

Slowly, one by one, the families bid farewell to their loved ones and left. Within hours, the old age home returned to its previous somber state. The once-animated elderly now sat silently, their faces heavy with unspoken sorrow. Like birds drenched in a monsoon downpour, they perched on the walls of the courtyard, gazing at the emptiness left behind.

The morning quiet, combined with the retreating noise of departing vehicles, only amplified the melancholy. "Our poor children," they whispered to each other. "How will they manage without us? What will they eat? How are they living without us? Poor things, they must be struggling."

The lively streams of their earlier days had turned into stagnant pools. Their hearts, once overflowing with joy at their children's footsteps, now ached as they watched them leave. The essence of motherhood, once celebrated as a divine gift, now trickled from their eyes as tears. Seeing this, even my own eyes welled up, unable to hold back the flood of emotions.

To Mother with Love

Mother! I'm coming to you, soaring through the skies with the wings of hope and eagerness. This eighty-year-old child is running with boundless energy to see you, the one who has gracefully embraced a hundred springs. I come to you, yearning for your presence, bowing to you with countless reverences.

My battalion—my wife, children, grandchildren, and great-grandchildren—will join us later for your birthday celebrations. But I couldn't wait. They may travel with me, but they cannot match my pace or longing.

I'm coming to sanctify the life you gifted me. With the courage you instilled in me, I've witnessed many victories. For eighty years, I've walked unwaveringly in the footsteps you set before me. With the inspiration you provided, I've never grown weary, nor have I ever strayed from the ideals you taught me.

From the moment I took my first breath, you nourished me with love and affection as if they were milk. When I took my first steps, you walked alongside me, correcting my stride. As my lips began to form words, you shaped my vocabulary. You became my shelter, giving me shade and comfort through life. You were my strength, my blessing, guiding me with wisdom and care. Even as you reach a hundred springs, you continue to be my guiding light.

Life threw many challenges at me, but when I faltered in the depths of despair, you reached out, pulled me up, and saved me. When hope seemed distant, you stood as a beacon of light before me. You taught me to turn struggles into strengths, to view hardships as stepping stones to success, and to cherish every victory without losing sight of humility.

From Krishna's wisdom to Rama's righteousness, Christ's compassion to Allah's boundless love, Buddha's peace to the patience and virtues of motherhood—you nurtured me with these divine qualities as if they were sweet morsels.

You instilled the essence of the five elements in me—earth's strength, water's tenderness, sky's vastness, fire's brilliance, and air's vitality. You crafted me as a reflection of these universal elements.

Among all my friends, you remain the truest companion. You are the first teacher who imparted wisdom and knowledge. Even when far away, you kept me alive with the thoughts of your love. Without hesitation, you fulfilled every wish of mine. You are my everything, my all.

I've earned immense name and fame, amassed wealth, and achieved recognition, but they all brought me temporary joy. The eternal treasure that has brought me lasting happiness is you.

You are a divine force, a perfect embodiment of womanhood. For your family, you've been a pillar of service. When tangled in life's challenges, your profound wisdom unraveled the knots effortlessly. You proved that true rest can only be found at your feet. Always keeping an eye on my well-being, you nourished me with unending love and care. You are the goddess of selfless giving, never asking for anything in return.

Once, you mentioned that you've had many birthdays, but you chose to make mine your own. By doing so, you gave my birth meaning. This time, as you celebrate your hundredth and I my eightieth, we are about to mark a milestone together. How many in this world are blessed with such fortune? Those who are, are truly divine.

Mother, I've never worshiped any deity. I've only revered them as ideals and honored their teachings in my life. In my eyes, no god surpasses the greatness of a mother. You have been my sole deity, one I've worshiped with my heart as a temple. My only desire has been to cherish and honor you.

You once said, "If you ever feel pride creeping into your heart, look at the vast sky and realize how small you are." From that moment, humility became my adornment. I've always considered myself a mere speck in the universe, and with that smallness, I now approach you for your blessings.

For your birthday, I wished to give you a gift that would bring you joy. After much thought, I decided that the best offering would be the experiences and memories we've shared. I've written a hundred letters, capturing every cherished moment. I plan to present them to you as a bouquet of love at your feet.

I'm certain you will accept them with kindness and bless me. With immense hope, I bring them to you, Mother.

On every birthday of mine, you've gifted me with something special. This time, for my eightieth, I wish to ask for a gift from you. I'm confident you will grant my wish.

"Live to see my hundredth birthday. Bless me even then." Grant me this one boon, Mother.

———•———

About the Author

Peesapati Chandra Sekhar, born in July 1955, is basically a short story writer. Most of his stories are prize winning. He worked as a lecturer for about three decades and now enjoying retirement life with family and friends. He Started his journey as a writer in 1981 and published many short stories in various magazines and recently his poems have been published in e-Journals. His Telugu Novel 'Soundarya Sikharam Amma' is published through Notion Press, Chennai.

'Mother - The Pinnacle of Beauty' is his first English Novel. The concept of universal motherhood is presented in this novel in a beautiful and poetic style. This book reminds every reader, his childhood memories with his mother. The main intention of writing this book is to drive everyone towards mother's realm and recollect his playful flash back.

Peesapati Chandra Sekhar
Kakinada
Andhra Pradesh, INDIA
Phone : +91 9966594999
Email : *peesapati.chandrasekhar@gmail.com*